Jamaica in 1850

———————

Jamaica in 1850

OR,

THE EFFECTS OF SIXTEEN YEARS
OF FREEDOM ON A SLAVE COLONY

John Bigelow

Introduction by Robert J. Scholnick

University of Illinois Press
Urbana and Chicago

First Illinois paperback, 2006
Introduction © 2006 by the Board of Trustees
of the University of Illinois
Originally published by G. P. Putnam, 1851
Manufactured in the United States of America
p 5 4 3 2 1
∞ This book is printed on acid-free paper.

Library of Congress Cataloging-in-Publication Data
Bigelow, John, 1817-1911.
Jamaica in 1850, or, The effects of sixteen years of freedom on a slave
colony / John Bigelow ; with an introduction by Robert J. Scholnick
  p.   cm.
Originally published: New York & London : Putnam, 1851. Includes
bibliographical references and index.
ISBN-13: 978-0-252-07327-4 (pbk. : alk. paper)
ISBN-10: 0-252-07327-4 (pbk. : alk. paper)
1. Jamaica—Description and travel. 2. Jamaica—Economic conditions.
3. Blacks—Jamaica—History—19th century. 4. Bigelow, John,
1817-1911—Travel—Jamaica.
I. Scholnick, Robert J. II. Title: Jamaica in 1850. IV: Title: Effects of sixteen
years of freedom on a slave colony.
F1871.B59   2006
972.92—dc22   2006003722

CONTENTS

EMANCIPATION AND THE ATLANTIC TRIANGLE

John Bigelow's *Jamaica in 1850*

———————

ROBERT J. SCHOLNICK

Even before its passage on August 29, 1833, the British Emancipation Act became a double-edged sword for American abolitionists, inspiring but fraught with danger if the "mighty experiment" of freeing some eight hundred thousand slaves in the West Indies should be judged a failure. The colonial secretary, Edward George Stanley, used the phrase "mighty experiment" in introducing the government's emancipation resolution to Parliament (Drescher, 123). Taking as an article of faith Adam Smith's dictum that slave labor is more expensive than free labor, British abolitionists expected that the "experiment" would yield such positive results that other nations would follow their lead. Most Americans, however, were quite content to wait until the evidence was in before acting. As the New York *Commercial Advertiser* observed on March 30, 1833, "The results which may follow the immediate emancipation of slaves in the West Indies may afford us the lesson of wisdom without the cost of experience" (Temperley, 113). But just who would evaluate emancipation? How would it be done? What mattered, the volume of sugar produced? Or was it the ability of former slaves to assume new lives as self-sufficient citizens? Whose story would be heard?

The Emancipation Act called for an apprenticeship period beginning in 1834 and ending in 1840, a time during which partially freed slaves would work approximately forty-five hours a week. Only in Antigua did freedom come immediately. Apprenticeship ended early, however, on August 1, 1838. As Sidney Mintz notes, "It was too much to ask that a man should be a slave on weekdays and a wage earner over the weekend" (206). Particularly in Jamaica, there followed a period of bitter conflict between determined, even brutal, planters and former slaves who struggled for autonomy (Holt, 79).

Charging that the British government had not provided adequate compensation for their slaves, planters complained as well that freedpersons refused to work except for exorbitant wages. In Jamaica, production of the primary export crop, sugar, fell some 23 percent during the apprenticeship period and declined substantially over the next ten years to less than half (49 percent) of preabolition levels (Holt, 119). In debt even before emancipation, many planters were forced to abandon their estates.

In 1846 Parliament approved Lord John Russell's plan for "admitting all foreign sugars, regardless of origin, at a uniform rate" (Temperley, 160-65, quotation on 160). The advantage in the British market previously given to crops from the British West Indies was eliminated. Henceforth, free-grown sugar had to compete with slave-grown crops from Cuba and Brazil. The slave traffickers now had increased incentives to bring in additional slaves—despite the British blockade of Africa. Even progressive British periodicals came to ask just what emancipation had accomplished. American abolitionists found themselves on the defensive because their opponents had only to cite the consequences of British emancipation to counter antislavery campaigns. Emancipation, slavery's apologists charged, had been as bad for the blacks, who were reverting to barbarism, as for planters and consumers. The prosperity of slaveholders in Brazil, Cuba, and the United States seemed to demonstrate that Adam Smith had erred in asserting that "the work done by slaves . . . is in the end, the dearest of any" (Drescher, 21).

That American abolitionists found themselves on the

defensive is reflected in the prefatory letter that Wendell Phillips added to *The Narrative of the Life of Frederick Douglass* in 1845: "In 1838, many were waiting for the results of the West India experiment, before they could come into our ranks. Those 'results' have come long ago; but, alas! few of that number have come with them, as converts. A man must be disposed to judge of emancipation by other tests than whether it has increased the produce of sugar . . . before he is ready to [begin] his anti-slavery life" (Douglass, 10). Phillips welcomed Douglass's *Narrative* as a moving story of heroic resistance and achievement. Similarly, *Jamaica in 1850*, John Bigelow's report of his visit to the island, became vitally important in the antislavery struggle. Better than anyone else, Bigelow rebuts those who used the decline in sugar production as evidence of racial inferiority. He, too, tells of heroic black resistance and achievement.

Bigelow argues that Jamaica's economic collapse was caused not by the alleged incapacity of former slaves but rather by the incompetence of largely absentee plantation owners functioning within a dysfunctional colonial system. It was not that former slaves refused to work but that lazy planters were neglectful managers. Adam Smith's dictum had not been disproved, but the sound principles of political economy—free trade, democracy, and economic opportunity and education for all—had not been tried at all. A founder of the Free-Soil Party in 1848, Bigelow appealed to that large group of Americans who disliked slavery but were fearful of ending it. He would propose that a revitalized Jamaica be invited to join the Union as a free state. It was a radical proposition indeed. A black majority state would enter the Union alongside South Carolina.

Published in New York, *Jamaica in 1850* is an American book that deals with a British question that had profound significance for America. It appeared just as the two nations were moving closer together in multiple ways. In 1846, under the Walker Tariff Act, America had reduced its restrictive tariffs even as Britain altered its protective agricultural policies. That year the two nations resolved their dispute over the Oregon boundary. On June 4, 1851, the *Times of London* claimed, "For all practical purposes the United States are far more closely united with this kingdom than any one of our colonies" ("Great Britain and America," 4).

Progressives in both countries realized that the cause of reform was indivisible. America would have to eliminate slavery if it were to serve as a model of democratic change for Britain, and Britain would have to improve conditions for its working class in order to creditably promote the antislavery cause. At the same time, British and American conservatives looked across the water for support. Hanging in the balance was the future of liberal democracy.

British Emancipation: A Double-Edged
Sword for American Abolitionists

In 1836 the American Anti-Slavery Society sent James
A. Thome and J. Horace Kimball to the West Indies to
demonstrate the truth of Adam Smith's dictum on free
labor. Their report, *Emancipation in the West Indies: A Six
Months' Tour,* appeared in 1838. Destined to become an
"antislavery best-seller in the United States," the book
asserted that because emancipation already should be
considered a success, America should follow the British
lead (Temperley, 91n83). The young writers found the most
determined resistance in Jamaica, where planters "had
sworn eternal hostility to every scheme of emancipation."
The "atrocities" practiced by the "masters and magistrates"
were nothing short of "appalling." Nevertheless, Thome and
Kimball claimed that "the *degree* of the failure" was "not so
great as had been represented" (108).

On the basis of success in Antigua, where production of
sugar increased slightly, the society changed its position
from "immediate emancipation, gradually accomplished"
to insist on *"immediate emancipation." Emancipation in the
West Indies* caused a "revolution in anti-slavery doctrine. To
such as were anxious to believe, it proved by example that
immediate emancipation was safe, practicable, and efficient"

(Barnes, 138-39, emphasis in the original). Both abolitionists and slavery's apologists saw that the battle over the meaning of British emancipation constituted a critical arena in the struggle over American slavery.

Representative of those the antislavery forces hoped to bring around was the author of an extended essay, "On the State of the West Indies before Emancipation," published in October 1838 in the *Princeton Review*, the conservative Presbyterian quarterly. Reflecting the optimism of the times, the reviewer, most likely its editor, Charles Hodge, asserted that "the great event of the present century is the emancipation of the slaves in the British Colonies. It is one of those social revolutions which, at intervals, form distinct eras in the history of our race" (602). Assuring readers that he had not become an abolitionist, the author insisted that the Bible does not prohibit slavery and that the institution cannot be considered immoral because slaveholders "were admitted to the Christian Church by the inspired apostles." Still, the early reports from the West Indies led him to claim that America would benefit enormously if slavery were eliminated because social improvement "is incompatible with the long continuation of slavery" (605). The Founders understood that "arbitrary power in the hands of sinful men is an evil, though at times necessary; that liberty is in itself a good, though at times unsustainable." Formerly, the South had been "quite as open and decided as the North in considering slavery a great social and political evil, rendered necessary, as they supposed, for the time being, by their peculiar circumstances," but now Southerners speak of slavery as a positive good (607). Nothing could do more to undermine the white South's hardening position than continued success in the West Indies. Noting the absence of violence since the beginning of apprenticeship, stable agricultural production, and the willingness of freedpersons to embrace Christianity, the writer insisted that "the prosperity of the islands has not been seriously diminished. . . . Those beautiful islands now raise their verdant plains and lofty mountains, covered with a free population in the infancy of civilization and Christian knowledge. . . . We look with cheerful confidence to their yearly progress in intelligence, prosperity, and virtue" (644).

Had those reports been forthcoming, slavery's apologists would have lost their prime argument, that blacks could not succeed in freedom. And that is precisely why such American apologists as Edmund Ruffin attempted to discredit free black communities in the United States as well (Ely, 196ff). Sadly, what we might now term as a campaign of "disinformation" seems to have succeeded, as Wendell Phillips recognized in introducing Douglass's *Narrative*. There was far more to the story than the amount of sugar produced, but there was no one to tell that story.

American abolitionists became anxious about the

absence of accounts in the press touting the success of emancipation. Arriving at the 1840 meeting of the World Antislavery Conference in England, they implored their hosts to generate glowing stories for use at home. Phillips for one urged British antislavery leaders to see to it that the "sentiments of the [British] nation" be articulated in its periodicals, which circulated widely in America (British and Foreign Anti-Slavery Society, 129-33; Temperley, 91). Instead, British writers told of plummeting production and demoralized planters. Coming even from journals that had supported emancipation, such accounts were devastating. A writer in *Blackwood's Magazine* in June 1844, James Macqueen, lamented that "instead of supplying her own wants with Tropical produce, and next nearly all Europe, as [Britain] formerly did, it is the fact that, in some of the most important articles, she has barely sufficient to supply her own wants; while the whole of her colonial possessions . . . are . . . supplied with—and, as regards the article of sugar, are consuming—foreign slave produce." It was a condition that, the writer warned, "cannot continue" (742).

American apologists now possessed the seemingly irrefutable evidence they needed. John C. Calhoun, then serving as secretary of state, drew from the *Blackwood's* article in telling French and British diplomats that "slave trade abolition and emancipation had cost the British people

$250 million and put twice that much capital at risk in the British West Indies" (Drescher, 171). Arguing that the Constitution established slavery, Calhoun warned the British not to interfere with the impending annexation of Texas as a slave state. In "Annexation of Texas," published that October, the *Southern Quarterly* quoted extensively from *Blackwood's* to gloat that the British "experiment of emancipation of the slaves . . . has not succeeded" but rather "resulted in total failure." The accounts from the West Indies stand as "melancholy dissuasives [*sic*] against these fatal errors. They teach patience and soberness, and warn us . . . to try no more experiments, with no better lights than we have at present before us" (509).

The transition from slavery to freedom in the West Indies would have been difficult under the best of circumstances. The determined resistance of Jamaican planters, however, further undermined the process. Before emancipation, slaves lived rent-free in "huts or tenements supplied by their owners and they had been allowed to cultivate estate backlands," but "as free wage workers they were asked to pay rents for huts and land, and ex-master and ex-slaves faced each other as landlord employers and employees" (Mintz and Hall, 770-71). Attempting to control their workers, planters seized "the houses and provision grounds that the apprentices had occupied gratis during slavery" (Holt, 134). In large numbers, freedpersons abandoned the huts and farms that by custom had "belonged" to them and they had been able to "bequeath." Remarkably, many were able to settle on Crown property; others purchased land from "ruined estates or the surpluses of economically viable estates" (Mintz, 159). Also important was the work of Baptist and Methodist missionaries in purchasing ruined estates for conversion into independent villages. "Between 1838 and 1844, nineteen thousand freedmen and their families removed themselves from the estates, bought land, and settled in free villages. In terms of the total population affected, this figure may represent an aggregate of as many as a hundred thousand persons" (Mintz, 160). On their farms, freed persons worked out a new way of life. "The material needs of daily living would be met by personal effort and because of personal motivation; the hated compulsion of the planter was no longer a spur to effort, and the freedman easily learned to live without it" (Mintz, 209).

As Howard Temperley observes, however, it was impossible "to convince anyone accustomed to regarding sugar production as the natural index of West Indian prosperity that the situation was not as bad as the planters said it was. Unlike trade figures, greater personal freedom and improved living conditions, real though they were to those who experienced them, were not susceptible to quantitative measurement"

(116). In the wake of the economic deterioration after 1838 even progressive British periodicals came to write critically of emancipation. After all, by 1840 "consumers were paying nearly 60 percent more for their sugar than the average price during apprenticeship, itself a 40 percent rise over the years of slavery" (Drescher, 158). In "Sugar and Slavery," republished by *Littell's Living Age* on July 20, 1844, the *Spectator* charged that "the public paid for Emancipation, and a badly-fulfilled bargain; it has paid long for 'slave trade suppression,' as the fruitless and costly *efforts* to suppress the slave trade are called; it pays a high price for sugar, to protect the West Indies from ruin, which is not done. . . . The public has been passive, in buying at any price the luxury of sentiment [even though] there is as much slavery as ever." During June and July of 1844 alone, *Littell's Living Age,* the Boston weekly, republished this and ten similar essays from British periodicals. When in 1846 Parliament passed the Sugar Duties Act the nation seemed to concede that the goals of emancipation—to free slaves while increasing production—would not be achieved. Antislavery journals angrily condemned the action but to no avail (Drescher, 174; Temperley, 161).

In 1848 a group of southern legislators led by Calhoun claimed that as disastrous as emancipation had been, it "furnishes a very faint picture of the calamities [abolition] would bring on the South" that speedily would be "overspread" by "wretchedness, and misery, and desolation" (Benton, 1:734-35). Thomas Carlyle's "Occasional Discourse on the Negro Question," published in *Fraser's* in December 1849 and republished in *Littell's Living Age* on February 9, 1850, was a heavy blow. The respected British writer depicted "Quashee," lolling lazily about the pumpkin patch while valuable crops were rotting. Charging that the laws of supply and demand "have an uphill task of it with such a man," Carlyle warned that "the idle black man in the West Indies had not long since the right, and will again if it please Heaven have the right . . . to be *compelled* to work as he was fit and to *do* the Maker's will" (250). This was interpreted in both Britain and America as a threat to compel former slaves to return to work on plantations, in effect to return them to a condition very much like slavery.

Responding in *Fraser's* the next month, John Stuart Mill correctly predicted the damage Carlyle's essay would do in America, where "the words of English writers of celebrity are words of power on the other side of the ocean. . . . I hardly know of an act by which one person could have done so much mischief." Mill challenged Carlyle's claims of innate racial inferiority and criticized him on the meaning of work. There is nothing inherently noble, Mill said, about producing spices for Europeans. Because he had not visited the West

Indies, however, he was unable to report on the new lives being built by freed persons. He failed to question Carlyle's assertion that former slaves were now able to earn such high wages that, in Mill's words, they could "exist in comfort on the wages of a comparatively small quantity of work" (466). Operating on the assumption that there was a labor shortage, Mill supported proposals to import additional workers. Bigelow would challenge these assumptions.

Carlyle's essay prompted the *Democratic Review,* a prominent New York monthly, to claim in "Centralization," published that April, that "a powerful re-action has taken place in England in regard to [attitudes toward] the blacks," especially as reflected in "the leading writers and the press, influenced by the Government." Noting that the "utter ruin" of the West Indies was "known to all," the author endorsed Carlyle's "very bold stand in favor of re-enslaving the blacks, who are doubtless rapidly sinking into the state of cannibalism from which white influence raised them" (302, 304). That may strike us as extreme, but that September Congress passed the Compromise of 1850, which included the infamous Fugitive Slave Law.

The Making of an Antislavery Journalist and Activist

Born into a merchant family in 1817 in the Hudson River town of Malden, New York, John Bigelow early became a passionate Democrat. In 1833, as a student at Washington (later Trinity) College in Hartford, he was thrilled when President Andrew Jackson visited. In debates at Washington and at Union College in New York, where he transferred, he vigorously articulated the principles of the Democratic Party (Clapp, 10). At Union, Bigelow came under the influence of another visionary leader, Eliphalet Nott, the long-time college president who had been "preaching against" slavery since 1811 (Hislop, 403-5). Within a decade after he graduated in 1836 Bigelow found that his commitment to Nott's antislavery stand placed him in opposition to the party of Jackson, which under James K. Polk came to be controlled by slaveholding interests during the 1840s.

Bigelow, following in the path of many ambitious young men, went to New York. Admitted to the bar in 1838, he found the law neither lucrative nor intellectually stimulating. Underemployment, however, did have its benefits. There was time for reading and discussions with a widening circle of brilliant friends, including the future governor and presidential candidate Samuel Tilden, whose biography he would write. In 1841 the editor of the *Democratic Review*, John L. O'Sullivan, moved the monthly from Washington to New York. O'Sullivan became Bigelow's journalistic mentor, and Bigelow found a political, intellectual, and literary home in the "Young America" movement associated with the *Democratic Review* (Widmer, 27ff). Strongly nationalistic, these writers identified

with the reform wing of the "Democracy," as New York's
Democratic Party was known.

Both in the pages of the *Democratic Review* and in William
Cullen Bryant's *Evening Post,* Bigelow quickly made a name
for himself as a brilliant, wide-ranging analyst, someone who
could write acutely about politics, workers' rights, free trade,
Greek and Roman literature, prison reform, intellectual
history, and state constitutional reform among other subjects.
In "Territorial Aggrandizement," published in October
1845, he spoke of the power of the American democratic
ideal to influence other nations. But in this time of Manifest
Destiny, when the United States would shortly attack Mexico,
Bigelow cautioned against military adventures. Territorial
expansion should come about peacefully and voluntarily—
as he would propose with Jamaica (Bigelow, "Territorial
Aggrandizement," 243-48). In "The Reciprocal Influences
of the Physical Sciences and of Free Political Institutions"
he celebrated the United States as the superior model of a
nation-state (13). Citing Adam Smith, Bacon, and Luther as
the intellectual forebears of America, Bigelow claimed that
the nation's evident success came from a dynamic and open
culture that encouraged innovation and scientific inquiry and
prized religious freedom and democracy. He would measure
Jamaica against such values.

Before the Baltimore presidential nominating convention

in 1844 Bigelow and other New York Democratic leaders expected that Martin Van Buren would emerge as the nominee. After Van Buren equivocated over the annexation of Texas, however, the southern wing of the party, led by Calhoun, blocked the former president. Polk, a slaveholder, came away as the nominee. Even so, Bigelow, Tilden, and O'Sullivan established the *Morning News*, a daily, to make Polk better known in New York. Indeed, they claimed their advocacy was responsible for Polk's narrow victory in New York—and hence his election as president. The reformers—now known as Barnburners—expected Polk to funnel New York patronage through their hero, Silas Wright, a former senator and now the newly elected governor, who opposed slavery. But reflecting the emergence of slavery as the preeminent national issue, Polk favored the proslavery (and conservative) Hunker faction. It is ironic that Bigelow's work on the *Morning News* helped carry New York and the nation for Polk, whose policies he would oppose.

In 1848 the rival factions of New York's Democratic Party each sent delegations to the national convention, where they were offered a compromise under which they would share power equally—but only if each pledged to support the party's nominee, most likely Sen. Lewis Cass, who was friendly to the South. Bigelow and other antislavery New York Democrats elected to bolt and form the Free-Soil

Party. They nominated Van Buren for the presidency and the Massachusetts "Conscience Whig" Charles Francis Adams as his running-mate.

With "Free Soil, Free Speech, Free Labor, and Free Men" as their motto the Free-Soilers "demanded that the federal government commit itself *'not* to *extend, nationalize,* or *encourage,* but to limit, localize, and discourage Slavery'* by all constitutional means" (Spann, 169). The defection ensured a Whig victory. Eric Foner has written that most Free-Soilers were more concerned with protecting white labor from competition with blacks than with ending slavery. Bigelow, however, was "one of the few Barnburners to support equal suffrage in 1846" (315, 323).

Following the 1848 election, Bigelow faced a tough question: Were his disagreements with the Democratic Party so fundamental as to force him to leave? A solution offered itself in December 1848 when the antislavery William Cullen Bryant invited him to become associate editor of the *Evening Post.* With borrowed funds Bigelow purchased a one-third interest in the firm. His energy, skill, and business acumen dramatically improved both the quality and the profitability of the newspaper and its printing plant.

Bryant quickly realized that in Bigelow he had a most capable associate, so capable that he left the publication in Bigelow's hands for much of 1849 while he traveled. Bigelow

wrote hard-hitting editorials opposing the spread of slavery
and urging that it be outlawed in the District of Columbia.
He bemoaned the disproportionate political power of a
comparatively few slaveholders, supported the admission
of California to the Union as a free state, and insisted that the
Founders had not intended that slavery would be permanent.
Antislavery leaders such as Charles Sumner recognized that
in Bigelow they had a powerful ally. Still, the *Post,* which
adhered to the states' rights principles of the Democratic
Party, did not call for immediate emancipation. It sought to
prevent slavery's spread while attempting to strengthen the
hand of antislavery moderates in the South. Bryant's "natural
optimism of spirit" had convinced him that slavery would
gradually give way "of its own innate weakness before the
advance of free labor" (Floan, 25). On May 3, 1851, Emerson
advocated a similar position: "First, abrogate [the Fugitive
Slave] law; then proceed to confine slavery to slave states,
and help them effectually make an end of it" (370).

   "When I joined the New York *Evening Post,*" Bigelow
recalled, "we were constantly confronted with the assertion
from Southern statesmen that the negro was wholly unfit for
liberty, and the British islands of the Antilles were referred
to in proof of it. We were also told that the island of Jamaica
had gone back almost to barbarism since the Emancipation
Act" (*Retrospections,* 1:94-95). Bigelow realized that the only

way to explode such myths would be to report factually about actual conditions on Jamaica. After Bryant returned to New York from Europe in December 1849, Bigelow claimed his turn to travel. If he needed prompting to go to Jamaica, the appearance of Carlyle's "Occasional Discourse" would have provided it.

Politics and Travel: Free Soil, Free Labor, and Free Men in Jamaica

Bigelow set off for Jamaica determined to confront the several assertions or myths surrounding the collapse of the Jamaican economy: first, that emancipation had failed because the former slaves had regressed to sloth and barbarism; second, that despite the offer of generous wages the freedpersons refused to work; third, that if planters only had reliable workers, production would increase and bring prosperity; and, fourth, that the profitable expansion of slavery in Brazil and Cuba proved that the "mighty experiment" had failed. "What was at stake on both sides of the Atlantic" in 1850, Seymour Drescher has written, "was not just a grim present but also an immensely grimmer future" (192).

Ominously, slaveholders were increasing agricultural production through new technology, suggesting that the institution was far more resilient than had been thought. Where did the apparent repudiation of Adam Smith leave Bigelow, who had called *Wealth of Nations* "the *novum organum* of political economy"? There was no underestimating the stakes. British conservatives understood that the campaign for instituting something very much like slavery in the West Indies would help protect the institution in the United States, thereby buttressing the conservative cause in Britain. A slaveholding America could not push for reforms in Britain. Jamaica became a battleground in the great transatlantic struggle for reform.

Far from retreating from Adam Smith and political economy, Bigelow argued that only fundamental, even radical, reforms could bring revitalization. The work of Smith and such theorists as James Mill in *Elements of Political Economy* (1844) provided him with the necessary analytical tools. What were the island's human and natural resources? What would be the most efficient means of production, distribution, and exchange? Political economy removed race from the equation and claimed that the best decisions are made by those closest to the situation. In 1846, writing in the *Democratic Review*, Bigelow had credited Smith with having created "a new science" designed "to enable [humankind] more completely to realize all the fruits of [its] industry" ("Reciprocal Influences," 13). He could not have anticipated that in just a few years he would face the challenge of applying those principles to a failing colonial economy.

But so committed was he to Smith's progressive project that *Jamaica in 1850* might just as well have been entitled *Political Economy in 1850: The Challenge of Jamaica.*

In the volume's preface Bigelow disingenuously claims he had decided to travel "merely for recreation, with no thought of troubling the public about it" other than to send an occasional letter to the *Evening Post* (i). His persona is that of a busy New Yorker bent on escaping the frigid city for a tropical vacation; no political agenda is evident. As soon as he disembarked at Port Royal, however, Bigelow confronted such shocking evidence of physical decay and economic decline that it required explanation. How had a land so rich in potential been allowed to stagnate?

Bigelow came prepared. He had read all the relevant government reports and the standard histories, including Bryan Edwards's *The History, Civil and Commercial, of the British Colonies in the West Indies* (1793), which was "well known in the United States" (127). Although Edwards conceded the damaging effects of slavery, in the end he defended the institution (Lewis, 553). Further, Bigelow, as a journalist, knew how to identify and cultivate the best sources, notably liberals within the governing class. He quoted in full a letter to the *Colonial Standard* from William Wemyss Anderson, an attorney who had traveled in the United States. Anderson articulated the argument

Bigelow developed: Poor management was responsible for the economic collapse. Bigelow's most important sources, it would seem, however, were members of the freeborn brown community, particularly Richard Hill, a distinguished naturalist and magistrate.

The power of Bigelow's narrative in this volume comes from his ability to support his arguments with precise observations of human activity placed in well-realized settings. Here is his description of women and children coming into town to market produce: "One of the most interesting spectacles to be witnessed about Kingston, is presented on the high road through which the market people, with their donkies, in the cool of the morning, pour into the city from the back country. They form an almost uninterrupted procession four or five miles in length" (117). It is as if the procession itself leads the reader to Bigelow's conclusion: "One may readily perceive how strong and universal must be the desire of the poor laborers to exchange their servile drudgery, on the lands of others, for this life of comparative ease and independence" (117). Such statements were, of course, meant to assure Americans anxious about the possible dangers of ending slavery.

In their ability to establish themselves as independent farmers the former slaves became heroic protagonists in Bigelow's narrative; the antagonists are planters and their defenders in Britain, particularly Carlyle and the colonial secretary, Lord Stanley, who had written a report justifying absentee ownership because the tropics posed unacceptable health risks to whites. Bigelow demolished that claim as well as Stanley's other major points. "On the whole," he observed, "the negro laborer has retrograded" following emancipation and "indolence, not industry, has been the result of his freedom" (129n). Stanley had come to function very much as the agent of the planters in the Foreign Office (Holt, 199).

Bigelow credits the British with having gotten it right in one area. Although not the case in the United States, in Jamaica it was common for people of all races to associate comfortably with each other. Anyone "accustomed to the proscribed condition of the free blacks in the United States will constantly be startled at the diminished importance attached here to the matter of complexion," although growing divisions existed between the "negroes or Africans, and the browns" who "shun all connection by marriage with the former, and experience no more unpardonable insult, than to be classified with them in any way" (25). Legal equality is a necessary condition for social and economic progress, but it is not sufficient. High-property qualifications for voting and serving in the assembly resulted in the planters controlling public policy and thwarting needed reforms. Bigelow's verdict—that Jamaica, despite appearances, was far from being a functioning democracy—has been confirmed by historians (Holt, 217).

Bigelow understood that the more graphic he was in describing economic decline in Jamaica, the more ammunition he would supply to American apologists. Nevertheless, he was unsparing. Property values had plummeted, and "poverty and ruin" were everywhere. The extent of the "financial reverses of this gem of the ocean" could be realized only by understanding its "exceeding fertility and unequalled natural resources," which Bigelow then enumerated. The central question concerned whether "human agency [could] extend any relief, and if any, what is it?" (70). Here Bigelow looked to the achievements of freed persons who at great personal sacrifice purchased small plots to cultivate "economically and intelligently." Far from reverting to barbarism, they were making sound economic decisions, and their productivity demonstrated what was now possible.

Bigelow's observations support the findings of those later scholars, including Sidney Mintz, who have emphatically rejected the view that the "adaptations of the ex-slaves were the result of a low level of economic aspirations, reflected deficient skills, or were evidence of regression to an African past" (Holt, 149). On the contrary, freedpersons, who were entrepreneurial before emancipation, were adapting well to the new economy. "On a patch of less than two acres, owned by a negro," Bigelow writes, was to be seen "the bread fruit, bananas, yams, oranges, shadducks, cucumbers, beans, pine-apple, plantain and chiramoya, besides many kinds of shrubbery and fruits of secondary value" (116). Astonished to discover that "the number of these colored proprietors is already considerably over hundred thousand, and constantly increasing," Bigelow charged that planters "discourage" land sales to the "blacks in every possible way, for they say that it raises the price of labor by increasing the independence of the laboring classes" (116, 118). But planters were unable to thwart the drive for independence.

Bigelow explicitly challenged Carlyle, whose assertions on race were "calculated to destroy all hope of ever bringing the blacks within the pale of an exalted civilization" (123). Further, the so-called exorbitant wages offered by planters were totally inadequate, contradicting both Carlyle and Mill. The "fact is, the negro cannot live on such wages, unless he owns in fee, a lot of three or five acres" (126). Forget about race, the real question was how to improve productivity: "Let labor be rewarded as it is in the United States or even in England, and let it be used with the same economy, and the face of Jamaica would change" (138).

To Bigelow's American eye, most planters failed to make efficient use of the workers who were available, and estates engaged in other inefficient practices such as owning their own sugar mills. These operated only part of the year and only part of the day. The central mills that Bigelow recommended, in contrast, could run around the clock. He did not report that Cuban planters were doing just that and, ironically, by importing advanced British machinery—often from British planters facing bankruptcy (Dresser, 186). Operational efficiencies enabled the Cubans to undercut British sugar. In Jamaica, central mills would not be established until late in the century, and then "progress was slow, despite legislative changes intended to facilitate this form of organization" (Holt, 369).

Arguing that Jamaica's reliance on staple crops for export placed it in a vulnerable position, Bigelow recommended that the government encourage farmers to find new opportunities by growing fruits and vegetables for the New York market, where they were in short supply in winter. To do that, the large estates would have to be subdivided, but Jamaicans would not adopt such sensible suggestions until the concluding third of the century, when a dramatic expansion of the fruit trade provided "unprecedented prominence to peasant agriculture" (Holt, 347). Bigelow also advised that Jamaica move to self-sufficiency by producing locally such necessities as lumber, fish, and wheat, which were being imported at high prices.

Bigelow's prediction that "nothing is more probable, in respect to the political fate of the island, twenty years hence, than that it will be one of the United States of America" (161) might well be read as a disguised manifestation of American imperialism. Because Bigelow saw the United States as the world's leading democracy and expected that slavery would be abolished, he believed that Jamaica would make far more progress if the island broke free of its colonial status and looked to the United States as a trading partner and political model. There is nothing of force or compulsion in Bigelow's statement, however, and it should be contrasted with the filibustering activities in Cuba of his former journalistic mentor John L. O'Sullivan. In 1851 O'Sullivan would be arrested in New York for violating the Neutrality Act by supporting a military expedition aimed at overthrowing the Cuban government so the island could become a slave state (Sampson, 216). In contrast, Bigelow's vision of a black-majority Jamaica entering the Union as a free state represented a challenge to American racism, which, as supported by ethnographic "science," held that "other races were incapable of reaching the level of the white race" (Horsman, 148).

The question of statehood aside, it is unfortunate that no group, whether in Jamaica or Britain, pushed for the fundamental reforms that Bigelow outlines in this book. No other contemporary observer had such keen insight into what had to be done to revive a failing economy and support freedpersons. Bigelow, in connecting political freedom and education to economic development, anticipated the approach of such progressive economists as Amartya Sen, who argues that freedom is a "causally effective factor in generating rapid change" (297).

Bigelow says nothing about the important work of dissenting missionaries in helping former slaves to purchase farms and yet that support was of great importance in the move toward independence that Bigelow describes. While he was in Jamaica, Bigelow heard rumors that the Haitian emperor, Faustin Soulouque, had begun persecuting brown citizens, causing many to flee, some to Jamaica. Bigelow met with one such refugee, whose complaints he reported. He dismissed these complaints, however, as overblown (28). He also includes, as an appendix, a report from a young Frenchman of a "Visit to the Emperor of Haiti," which put the situation in the best possible light. Bigelow should have trusted the Haitian refugee; the emperor, who deployed various paramilitary groups against his opponents, had a rule that was notably bloody and corrupt (Rotberg, 83-84). Bigelow's misreading grew from his determination to support the antislavery cause; he would visit Haiti some three years later to report firsthand on that island.

"The Democratic Horror of Black Blood": Responses to Jamaica in 1850 in Britain and America

When Bigelow returned to New York in early March he faced stiffening resistance to the antislavery cause. On March 7 Daniel Webster delivered "The Constitution and the Union," an address the *Post* fiercely attacked as a sell-out to the slave power (Clapp, 71). The desire to preserve the Union had come to trump antislavery feeling in many circles in the North. Bigelow's former colleagues at the *Democratic Review* published "Centralization" that April, which cited Carlyle's "Occasional Discourse" to claim that the British were now coming around to support the American position on slavery. In June, New Orleans's *DeBow's Review* prefaced its reprinting of the Carlyle essay with an assertion that "the West India question is for the first time put in its true light" (527). It was against this darkening atmosphere that Bigelow's dispatches appeared in the *Post,* the first on February 20 and the concluding installment on May 24.

Antislavery Americans faced a daunting challenge. As John Greenleaf Whittier wrote in responding to Carlyle in the *National Era* on May 2, "It is difficult to treat sentiments so atrocious, and couched in such offensive language with anything like respect." He feared that "our anti-Christian prejudices against the colored man might be strengthened and confirmed by [Carlyle's] malignant vituperation and sarcasm" (1-4). In Britain, Carlyle's essay "signalized the emergence of a new and particularly ugly form of racism" (Rice, 330-31).

Just when antislavery leaders needed transatlantic support more than ever, the apparent British retreat was discouraging. Were the British fearful that abolition would threaten their supply of cotton? The *Post* came under attack from the New York state Democratic Party and from Tammany Hall "for its uncompromising resistance to the extension of slavery," as it reported on March 14, 1850. The passage of the Compromise Act of 1850 provoked mob attacks on abolitionists in northeastern cities. On the other side, New York senator William Henry Seward spoke on March 11, 1850, of a "higher law" than a constitution that recognized slavery. Abolitionists began to form vigilance committees to save fugitive slaves from capture.

As soon as they began to appear, Bigelow's dispatches in the *Post* attracted attention, as reviewers of the published volume would note. On March 23, *Littell's Living Age* began serializing them, and while preparing the book for publication Bigelow strengthened and expanded his arguments. Most important, he added the uncompromising response to Carlyle in chapter 13. The book, which George P. Putnam released on Monday, October 28, was an account of what Bigelow actually saw and an attempt to counter the hardening of the proslavery position.

The Putnam firm was known for travel books, but Bigelow's work was sold as a treatment of the most pressing social problem that faced Americans (Greenspan, 250). The volume drew impassioned reviews from both the pro and antislavery camps, and, significantly, a number of reviewers not identified with either side responded positively to Bigelow's economic arguments.

On November 14, 1850, a full-page review in Horace Greeley's *Daily Tribune* weighed in on the question of race: "In the course of his argument, the author has occasion to refer to the extravaganzas of Carlyle on the subject of West India Slavery, and inflicts on that writer a summary chastisement." The review described *Jamaica in 1850* as primarily a "treatise on Political Economy . . . rather than a book of travels, or a record of personal incidents." Still, "It cannot be read without interest" (6). Given the extensive circulation of the *Tribune* throughout the Northeast and into the Ohio Valley, Bigelow had reason to be pleased. Similarly, on November 28, 1850, in a wide-ranging discussion, the *National Era* commended Bigelow for publishing "the best work concerning the present condition of Jamaica" (191). Such commercial New York newspapers as the *Journal of Commerce* and *Courier and Inquirer* were also positive, and in December 1850 *Harper's New Monthly* affirmed Bigelow's thesis that "the root of the evil . . . is to be found [not in the former slaves, but] in the non-residence of the landholders, encumbered condition of real estate, and the monopoly of the soil by a small number of proprietors" (140).

One finds, however, ambivalence on the question of race, even among those who wrote positively of *Jamaica in 1850*. That is evident, for instance, in a discussion from February 1851 in the *New Englander and Yale Review,* a "magazine devoted to expressing the views of free Christian men and women," as its proprietor E. R. Tyler wrote in the 1843 prospectus (1). The reviewer recognized that Bigelow raised important questions: Are "the inferior races of men" destined to "become extinct by the necessary progress of the superior races?" Or, is it possible that "by the divine influences of Christianity, they are to be elevated and brought to stand on the same level with the most civilized nations?" Will they "by intermarriage" become some other race. No answers were given even though *Jamaica in 1850* was praised as "by far the best" of the books on Jamaica (155). Bigelow prompted a reconsideration of racist assumptions.

Proslavery journals recognized the need to respond, and the *Democratic Review* delivered an extensive rebuke in December. Drawing from Bigelow's own descriptions, it claimed that "a completely savage state is being rapidly approximated" on the island. The culprits were former slaves, who "will not work." Ignoring Bigelow's report that former slaves were making exceptional progress, the reviewer insisted that for blacks to attempt to achieve anything beyond mere subsistence would "do violence against their nature." Bigelow's prediction that Jamaica would join the Union induced the reviewer to apoplexy, describing "the complete inferiority [of the black] to the white race, and its utter incapacity to maintain by itself the state of civilization, to which it has been advanced by white aid" (496). Abolition posed a dire threat to this "great and glorious nation." Americans of Anglo-Saxon descent had built a nation "upon a soil, previously occupied for countless ages, by a race who never improved it."

It is a short step from the *Democratic Review*'s justification of dispossession and extermination of Indians to its justification of slavery. Only when placed "under the direction of the whites" would blacks make "progress both physically and mentally." If slavery were to be abolished, "a rapid retrogression would result, until the blacks, having receded to the savage state of the aborigines, would be displaced and exterminated" ("Jamaica," 496).

Southern periodicals similarly attacked *Jamaica in 1850,* arguing that the economic difficulties of the West Indies provided evidence of racial inferiority. The *Southern*

Quarterly commented that "the African race seems to have stood still, and only to have emerged from its profound barbarism and ignorance when brought in contact with and under the subjection of the white" ("Emancipation in the British West Indies," 444).

The most curious response came from the *North American* in October 1851. In a wide-ranging essay on "Slavery in the United States," it revealed the tortured moral reasoning of the "Cotton Whig" community of Boston and Cambridge, in particular the contradictions of Harvard moral philosophy. As Daniel Walker Howe has written, "The slavery problem brought to the fore the basic contradiction between Unitarian ethical thought, which taught the limitless perfectibility of every person, and Harvard 'civil policy,' which praised a stable and hierarchical society" (271). The reviewer conceded that slavery was evil but could not think of a way to eliminate it because he could not envision an America where races live side by side as equals. The only solution, the reviewer maintained, was colonization. The fact that millions of Irish and Germans had crossed the ocean to come to America was proof that large populations could transfer themselves in the other direction, whether back to Africa or down to Jamaica. Had not Bigelow demonstrated that free blacks could do well on that fertile island?

In his *Retrospections* Bigelow recalled that *Jamaica in*

1850 "sold very rapidly and attracted considerable attention in England" (1:95). Yet the book was not widely reviewed; neither the *Spectator* nor the *Times* did so, nor did *Chambers'* or *The Athenaeum*. Only one review is listed in the *Wellesley Index*, that in the *Edinburgh Review* of April 1859. The comparative lack of reviews can be explained by the fact that the book did not have a British publisher. The title page identifies "W. C. Bryant & Co." as its printers. Because most of the material already had been set in type at the *Post*— and given the urgency in getting the book in print—such an arrangement made sense. Typically, however, Putnam contracted with one of several well-established New York printers for his books (Greenspan, 215). It would seem that Putnam acted more as distributor than publisher. On May 4, 1851, Bigelow would note in his *Journal* that he still had approximately one hundred copies on hand (Clapp, 70).

The need to get the book into print quickly meant that neither Bigelow nor Putnam had time to secure a British publisher or arrange for the book to be printed in Great Britain, something that was necessary for a volume to receive copyright protection. By way of contrast, Bryant's *Tales of a Traveller,* also published in 1850 by Putnam, was brought out in London by Richard Bentley, also the publisher of Herman Melville's *Moby-Dick,* which was published in England in October 1851.

Even though the title page of *Jamaica in 1850* identifies New York and London as the cities of publication, it was not considered a British book. *The British Catalogue* lists only New York as the place of publication, and each review lists New York as the city of publication. Yet there is no reason to doubt Bigelow's assertion that the book was well received in Britain.

Bigelow recalled that "Mr. [Albany] Fonblanque, then editor of the *Examiner*," wrote about it in several articles "which he employed with effect in defense of the English policy of emancipation, adopted only sixteen years before" (*Retrospections*, 1:95). Remarkably, *The Examiner*, the "chief organ of high-class intellectual radicalism" (Davies, 363-65), published its first discussion of Bigelow's Jamaican trip, "Prospects of Jamaica," on June 1, 1850. Having read the dispatches in the *Post*, Fonblanque praised Bigelow as an "acute and traveled American," someone who "sees at a glance what the proprietors cannot see, that their real want of success is not owing to the dearness of wages or loss of protection, but to their indolence, want of enterprise, and unskilfulness" (339). *The Examiner* published as well excerpts from Bigelow's letters. In Boston, *Living Age* reprinted Fonblanque's essay on August 10, 1850, strategically placing it following the last of its own republication of Bigelow's dispatches.

British progressives such as Fonblanque saw that Bigelow offered just what they needed—ammunition to respond to the racist voices heard with increasing frequency following Carlyle's article in *Fraser's*. In February 1851, for instance, in "The Dangers of the Country," *Blackwood's* blamed black inferiority for the collapse of the West Indies: "Jamaica, Demerara, and India, *might* have furnished cotton enough for all our wants. Why, then, do they not do so? . . . We have ruined the West Indies by emancipating the negroes, and then admitting foreign sugar all but on the same terms as our own, and therefore cotton cannot be raised to a profit in those rich islands—for *continuous* labor, of which the emancipated negroes are incapable, is indispensable to its production" (216).

Most likely the book was actually sold in London by Putnam's energetic British agent John Chapman, who was both publisher and bookseller (Greenspan, 215). Chapman, who in October 1851 would purchase the *Westminster Review*, occupied a commodious establishment at 142 Strand, which served as his residence, his place of business, and also as a rooming house much favored by visiting Americans, including Emerson, Greeley, Bryant, and Putnam (Eliot, 8). Another border at this time was Marian Evans, "George Eliot," with whom Chapman was both romantically and professionally involved. Chapman's establishment, the scene of his famous soirees, had become "a focal point for uniting the scattered forces of liberalism" in Britain (Secord, 486).

A great champion of American writers, Chapman was the ideal person to promote and sell Bigelow's book. He wrote in his diary on February 9, 1851, that he tried to interest the editor of the *Edinburgh Review* in employing "Miss Evans of whom I spoke as a man proposing she should write . . . on Mackay, Martineau & Atkinson's book, on Slavery, or any subject . . . if within her province" (Eliot, 140). Nothing apparently came of the proposal, but the entry shows that the slavery question was much on his mind, and that of George Eliot, at just the time *Jamaica in 1850* would have come into his hands.

A laudatory review did appear the *Westminster Review* in April 1851. Explicitly responding to Carlyle and other racist voices, the author counters the myth that the blacks had regressed to barbarism: "The abolition of slavery seems to have had an excellent effect upon the negroes, who exhibit marked symptoms of improvement, while their former masters content themselves with idle lamentations on the 'good old times.' In the end, slavery eventually avenges the wrongs of the oppressed upon those who have profited by the atrocious crime." Moreover, "we have been much interested in the account Mr. Bigelow gives of the eagerness which the negroes exhibit to become small landed proprietors, in order that they may have votes for the Assembly" (Review of *Jamaica in 1850*). With biting irony the reviewer claims that even the few extracts provided would "serve to show that what the Jamaica landlords most require is, 'protection' from their own mismanagement and folly." However, "the habits produced by protection and slavery upon the planters, are eminently unfavorable to the business-like management of their property" (Review, 135-36). Was the review by Marian Evans?

Fonblanque's review in *The Examiner*, which appeared on April 5, 1851, was similarly acute and biting.

> We recognize in Mr. Bigelow the author of some excellent letters from Jamaica which appeared last year in an American newspaper, and on which we had ourselves to bestow a very hearty approbation. [The present volume] contains the most searching analysis of the present state of Jamaica, and, moreover, the most sagacious prognostications of the future prospects of the island, that have ever been published. Mr. Bigelow is an accomplished, acute, and liberal American. As such, an eye-witness and a participator of the greatest and most successful colonial experiment the world has ever seen, he is, necessarily, a better and more impartial judge of the subject he treats of than any Englishman of equal capacity and acquirement. Mr. Bigelow makes short and easy work of planters, attorneys, book-keepers, sophistries, and Stanleys. In doing so, his language is invariably that of a man of education and a gentleman. He might have crushed them with a sledge-hammer, but he effects his purpose as effectually with a pass or two of a sharp and polished small-sword. (212-13)

The Examiner's only point of disagreement was with Bigelow's prediction that Jamaica would join the Union as a state. American racism, Fonblanque maintained, was too deeply ingrained to allow for a black-majority state. He predicted that Jamaica would come to look to America in matters both of trade and social development (212-13). Again the review in *The Examiner* did double duty; *Living Age* reprinted it on May 31, 1851 (426-29). The two reviews alone would be enough to bring the book to the attention of progressive British readers.

Although the *Times of London* did not review the book, there is a telling reference to it in Samuel Phillips's extended discussion of *Uncle Tom's Cabin* on September 1, 1852 (also republished in *Living Age* on October 16, 1852). After drawing from Bigelow to report that "the manumitted slaves of Jamaica, are, in the sight of the law, in the estimation of their fellows, and in the eye of God, equals with those whose actual 'property' they were the other day," Phillips compared this "salutary state of things" with the "certain doom of the negro emancipated by his American master! The democratic horror of black blood knows no bounds. . . . What avail the pathetic appeals, the painful incidents, the passionate denunciations with which *Uncle Tom's Cabin* abounds, in the teeth of such facts as these?" (*Littel's*, 100).

Additional evidence of the book's lasting impression in

Great Britain comes from an extended essay on "The West Indies" published in the *Edinburgh Review* in April 1859. The liberal quarterly conceded that "the world" had long since reached the conclusion that emancipation had failed, that "our sugar colonies are as good as swept off the face of the earth" (423). In framing his response Charles Buxton drew extensively from Bigelow, whom he described as "an American traveler of great intelligence and observation" (437). *Jamaica in 1850* remained essential for progressive Britons throughout the decade.

In America, *Jamaica in 1850* figured in the ongoing debate. Apologists warned that were slavery to be abolished the horrors of Jamaica would be visited upon the South—but on a far greater scale. Edmund Ruffin condemned Bigelow as a "Northern Abolitionist and negrophilist" who erred in ascribing the condition of Jamaica to the "residence of the few remaining whites." Instead, "All Bigelow's facts go to prove these evils to be the result of the incurable indolence and improvidence of the freed negroes" (35). But the Abolitionist leader Lydia Maria Child drew extensively from Bigelow for her *The Right Way the Safe Way, Proved by Emancipation in the British West Indies, and Elsewhere* (1862).

Conclusion

When Bigelow set out for Jamaica in January 1850 the view that British emancipation had failed because of the alleged inferiority of blacks was widely held on both sides of the Atlantic. Bigelow brilliantly turned the tables by demonstrating that freedpersons had become productive citizens. It is, essentially, their story that he tells, and from their perspective, Emancipation was a resounding success. *Jamaica in 1850* was recognized as the best book that had been written on the topic to that date, and it has found a place among the important books written about the island. In 1936 Lord Sydney Haldane Olivier drew extensively from Bigelow for *Jamaica: The Blessed Island* and praised him as "an exceptionally well qualified American observer" (143).

In championing free soil, free men, and free labor Bigelow looked ahead to the campaign of Abraham Lincoln. By 1856 he had left the Democratic Party and produced a campaign biography of the Republican candidate John C. Frémont. In 1861 he sold his interest in the *Evening Post* and became the U.S. counsel-general and then ambassador in Paris, where he helped keep the French and other European powers from recognizing the Confederacy. While in France, Bigelow purchased the original holograph of Benjamin Franklin's *Autobiography* and published a notable edition of it in 1868. Like Franklin, Bigelow, who died on December 19, 1911, was a skilled and effective journalist, publisher, and diplomat. *Jamaica in 1850* is a brilliant expression of his commitment to freedom, democracy, and racial equality.

WORKS CITED

I first learned about Jamaica in 1850 from reading John Bigelow's dispatches to the *Post*, which Eliakim Littell reproduced in *Littell's Living Age*, the Boston weekly now available on-line through the Making of America project. Although the *Living Age* specialized in reprinting articles from British periodicals, Littell understood the crucial importance of Bigelow's work for the ongoing transatlantic dialogue on slavery. In order for American readers to appreciate its importance for British readers, he reproduced in full the *Examiner's* acute review of the volume, which had appeared on April 5, 1851. He included as well the work by Thomas Carlyle and John Stuart Mill cited below. All American periodicals cited are accessible on-line through Making of America.

[Allison, Archibald.] "The Dangers of the Country." *Blackwood's Magazine* 69 (Feb. 1851): 196-222.

"The Annexation of Texas." *Southern Quarterly* 6 (Oct. 1844): 483-520.

Barnes, Gilbert Hobbs. *The Antislavery Impulse, 1830-1844.* 1933. Reprint. Gloucester: Peter Smith, 1957.

[Benton, Thomas Hart]. *Thirty Years' View; or, A History of the Workings of the American Government for Thirty Years, from 1820 to 1850.* 2 vols. New York: D. Appleton, 1856.

Bigelow, John. *The Life of Samuel J. Tilden.* 2 vols. New York: Harper and Brothers, 1895.

———. "The Reciprocal Influences of the Physical Sciences and of Free Political Institutions." *Democratic Review* 18 (Jan. 1846): 13.

———. *Retrospections of an Active Life.* Vols. 1-3, New York: Baker and Taylor, 1909; vols. 4-5, Garden City: Doubleday, Page, 1913.

———. "Territorial Aggrandizement." *Democratic Review* 17 (Oct. 1845): 243-48.

———. *The Wit and Wisdom of the Haitians.* New York: Scribner and Armstrong, 1877.

British and Foreign Anti-Slavery Society. *Proceedings of the General Anti-Slavery Convention Called by the Committee of the British and Foreign Anti-Slavery Society, June 12–June 23, 1840.* London: The Society, 1841.

Buxton, Charles. "The West Indies, as They Were and Are." *Edinburgh Review* (April 1859): 421-60.

Carlyle, Thomas. "Occasional Discourse on the Negro Question." *Fraser's Magazine* 40 (Dec. 1849): 670-79. Reprinted in *Littell's Living Age*, March 9, 1850, 465-69.

"Centralization." *Democratic Review* (April 1850): 289-305.

Child, Lydia Maria. *The Right Way the Safe Way, Proved by Emancipation in the British West Indies and Elsewhere.* 1862. Reprint. Westport: Negro Universities Press, 1970.

Clapp. Margaret. *Forgotten First Citizen: John Bigelow.* 1947. Reprint. New York: Greenwood Press, 1968.

Douglass, Frederick. *The Frederick Douglass Papers, Series 2: Autobiographical Writings,* vol. 1: *Narrative of the Life of Frederick Douglass, an American Slave.* Edited by John Blassingame et al. New Haven: Yale University Press, 1999.

Drescher, Seymour. *The Mighty Experiment: Free Labor versus Slavery in British Emancipation.* New York: Oxford University Press, 2002.

Eliot, George. *The George Eliot Letters.* Edited by Gordon S. Haight. Vol. 1 of 9 vols. New Haven: Yale University Press, 1954-78.

Ely, Melvin Patrick. *Israel on the Appomattox: A Southern Experiment in Black Freedom from the 1790s through the Civil War.* New York: Alfred K. Knopf, 2004.

"Emancipation in the British West Indies." *Southern Quarterly Review* 7 (April 1853): 422-54.

Emerson, Ralph Waldo. *Emerson's Prose and Poetry.* Edited by Joel Porte and Saundra Morris. New York: W. W. Norton, 2001.

Floan, Howard R. "The *New York Evening Post* and the Ante-bellum South." *American Quarterly* 8 (1956): 243-53.

Foner, Eric. "Racial Attitudes of the New York Free-Soilers." *New York History* 46 (Oct. 1965): 311-29.

"Great Britain and America." *Times of London,* June 4, 1851, 4. Reprinted in *Littell's Living Age,* Aug. 28, 1851, 373.

Greenspan, Ezra. *George Palmer Putnam: Representative American Publisher.* University Park: Pennsylvania State University Press, 2000.

Haight, Gordon, ed. *George Eliot and John Chapman: With Chapman's Diaries.* New Haven: Yale University Press, 1940.

Harris, Sheldon H. "John Louis O'Sullivan and the Election of 1844 in New York." *New York History* 41 (July 1960): 278-98.

Hislop, Codman. *Eliphalet Nott*. Middletown: Wesleyan University Press, 1971.

[Hodge, Charles.] "On the State of the West Indies before Emancipation." *Princeton Review* 10 (Oct. 1838): 602-44.

Holt, Thomas C. *The Problem of Freedom: Race, Labor, and Politics in Jamaica and Britain, 1832-1938*. Baltimore: Johns Hopkins University Press, 1992.

Horsman, Reginald. *Race and Manifest Destiny: The Origins of American Radical Anglo-Saxionism*. Cambridge: Harvard University Press, 1981.

Howe, Daniel Walker. *The Unitarian Conscience: Harvard Moral Philosophy, 1805-1861*. 1970. Reprint. Middletown: Wesleyan University Press, 1988.

Lewis, Gordon. "Pro-Slavery Ideology." In *Caribbean Slavery in the Atlantic World*. Edited by Verene Shepherd and Hilary McD. Beckles, 544-79. Kingston: Ian Randall Publishers, 2000.

Macqueen, James. "Africa Slave Trade—Tropical Colonies." *Blackwood's Magazine* (June 1844): 731-48.

Mill, John Stuart. "The Negro Question." *Fraser's Magazine* 41 (Jan. 1850). Reprinted in *Littell's Living Age*, March 9, 1850, 465-69.

Mintz, Sidney W. *Caribbean Transformations*. 1974. New York: Columbia University Press, 1989.

———, and Douglas Hall. "The Origins of the Jamaican Internal Marketing System." In *Caribbean Slavery in the Atlantic World*. *Papers in Caribbean Anthropology* no. 57 (New Haven, 1970), 3-26. Reprint. *Caribbean Slavery in the Atlantic World*. Edited by Verene Shepherd and Hilary McD. Beckles, 758-73. Kingston: Ian Randle Publishers, 2000.

Olivier, Sydney Haldane. *Jamaica: The Blessed Island*. 1936. Reprint. New York: Russell and Russell, 1971.

Review of *Jamaica in 1850*. *The Examiner*, April 5, 1851, 212-13.

Review of *Jamaica in 1850*. *New Englander and Yale Review* 9 (Feb. 1851): 155.

Review of *Jamaica in 1850*. *Westminster Review* (April 1851): 135-36 [American ed.].

Rice, C. Duncan. "Literary Sources and British Attitudes to Slavery." In *Anti-Slavery, Religion and Reform: Essays in Memory of Roger Anstey*. Edited by Christine Bolt and Seymour Dresser, 330-31. Hamden: Archon USA, 1980.

Rotberg, Robert J. *Haiti: The Politics of Squalor.* Boston: Houghton Mifflin, 1971.

Ruffin, Edmund. "Equality of Races—Hatien and British Experiments." *DeBow's Review* (July 1858).

Sampson, Robert D. *John L. O'Sullivan and His Times.* Kent: Kent State University Press, 2003.

Secord, James. *Victorian Sensation: The Extraordinary Publication, Recpetion, and Secret Authorship of Vestiges of the Natural History of Creation.* Chicago: University of Chicago Press, 2000.

Sen, Amaratya. *Development as Freedom.* New York: Oxford University Press, 1999.

"Slavery in the United States: Its Ends, Alterations, and Remedies." *North American Review* (Oct. 1851): 347-86.

Spann, Edward K. *Ideals and Politics: New York Intellectuals and Liberal Democracy, 1820-1880.* Albany: SUNY Press, 1972.

"Sugar and Slavery." *The Spectator.* Reprinted in *Littell's Living Age*, July 20, 1844, 586-88.

Temperley, Howard. *British Antislavery: 1833-1870.* London: Longman, 1972.

Thome, James A., and J. Horace Kimball. *Emancipation in the West Indies: A Six Months' Tour.* New York: American Antislavery Society, 1838.

Tyler, E. R. "Prospectus." *New Englander and Yale Review* 1 (Jan. 1843): 1.

Walker, Daniel Howe. *The Unitarian Conscience: Harvard Moral Philosophy, 1805-1861.* 1970. Reprint. Middletown: Wesleyan University Press, 1988.

"The War against the South." *DeBow's Review* 8 (June 1850): 271-77.

Whittier, John Greenleaf. "Thomas Carlyle on the Slave Question." *National Era*, May 2, 1850, 1-4.

Acknowledgments

My William and Mary colleagues Terry Meyers and Melvin Patrick Ely provided careful readings of early versions of this introduction, and I am grateful for their efforts. Olywn Blouet of Virginia State University and James Walvin of

York University offered acute criticism, and an anonymous external reader for the University of Illinois Press also provided suggestions that were both supportive and challenging. Laurie Matheson, my acquisitions editor at the Press, has believed in this project from its outset, and Mary Giles helped improve the manuscript.

Jamaica in 1850

PREFACE

In the following pages the author has endeavored to explain the causes of the stricken and prostrate condition of one of the most delightful, and formerly, one of the most productive islands in the world, and to indicate the processes by which, in his judgment, the laws of nature and of trade are providing for the ultimate restoration of its ancient prosperity and wealth. They embrace the substance of observations made during a recent excursion to Jamaica, which, it is proper for him to say, was undertaken merely for recreation, and with no thought of troubling the public about it, except perhaps, by an occasional letter to the public journal with which he is professionally connected. During his absence he found occasion to address several communications respecting Jamaican affairs, to the readers of the *Evening Post,* and upon his return was pleased to discover that they had been the means, to some extent, of developing the lively curiosity which pervades the public mind of America, for information about the politico-economical condition of that island, after a deliverance of sixteen years from chattel slavery. That curiosity the author has endeavored to gratify, without attempting to do anything more. He has not presumed to write a history or a geography of Jamaica, nor to present a scientific statement of its resources, neither has he written a book of travels. He has limited the personal narrative almost exclusively to such incidents as seemed necessary to an intelligible analysis of the causes which have reduced Jamaica to her present deplorable condition, and of the means which are in operation for her ultimate restoration. He has endeavored to give a correct picture of Jamaica as she is, not what she has been; nor has he referred to her past history farther than was necessary for that purpose.

The views he has taken of the wants of Jamaica, and of the duty of the Home Government toward her, are essentially different from those professed, so far as he knows, by any political party either there or in England, and yet he publishes them with some confidence, for he is satisfied that they are such as almost any American would adopt, who should visit the island and inform himself with tolerable minuteness, of its physical an political condition.

The author avails himself on this occasion to make his grateful acknowledgements to those friends whose acquaintance, it was his privilege to make in Jamaica, and whose hospitable attentions enabled him to forget that he was nearly two thousand miles from his home, a stranger in a strange land. He desires also, specially to recognise his obligations to Captain J. D. Wilson, of the U.S. Mail Steamer *Empire City,* to whose devoted courtesy he owed many important privileges and facilities during his absence, and whose personal and professional character, it will always be his delight to honor.

NEW YORK, OCT. 21ST, 1850

JAMAICA IN 1850.

CHAPTER I.

Departure from New York—How to escape sea-sickness—Our
passengers—Taylor, cousin of General Zachary Taylor—The
Pass of Mayaguana—Arrival at Port Royal—Commodore
Brooks—Kingston seen from the Bay.

IT is not easy to imagine a more delightful series of
sensations than one experiences in passing at the rate of
two hundred and fifty miles a day, in a first class steam-
ship like the Empire City, from the rigors of a northern
winter, to the soft and genial temperature of the tropics.
It was the second day after New Year's, at precisely
three o'clock in the afternoon, that we sailed from pier No.
3, leaving New York city behind us all ice-bound, her
streets covered with snow and resonant with sleigh bells.
Furs and woollens enveloped her population, and thermo-
meters of every sect and denomination were agreed that
the weather was very cold. The greater part of the night
following that of our departure, I passed in walking the

1

deck of the steamer without an overcoat of any kind, and
was warm and comfortable, as if it were an evening in
June instead of January. In two days more linen clothing was gladly substituted by the less prudent of our company, including myself, for flannels, and the pitch trickled
from the seams of the ship, and from her rigging, under
the unrelenting heat of a tropical sun. But the air was
always pure, soft and exhilirating, the heat not in the least
enervating, and the effect of the gradual transition was not
unlike the delightful sensations of a warm bath, protracted
through a series of days instead of minutes. No stimu-
lants afford such delightful sensations. I had small occasion for sleep, to which I did not devote on an average
more than three hours out of every twenty-four, nor did I
suffer any inconvenience from the want of it. I always
awoke refreshed and hungry.

Neither was I sea-sick. I discovered soon after our departure the propriety of adopting the following precautions,
to which I presume I owe my exemption from this common terror of inexperienced sea voyagers. In the first
place, I was careful never while sitting in the cabin, to rest
my feet upon the floor, but always to stretch them upon
the sofa or a chair; in the next place, I always seated
myself so that the roll of the ship should pitch me from
side to side, and not forward and backward. In the third
place, whenever I felt in the least unsettled, I was careful

never to fix my attention upon any near object, and especially avoided reading or writing; if necessary, I closed my eyes altogether. Finally, I made it a point to go regularly to the table and eat moderately of plain food. By the careful observance of these precautions, I was enabled to enjoy my voyage without interruption, and I came to the conclusion that most persons, if in good health when they embark, may avoid sea-sickness altogether by following my example.

In six days from the period of our departure we were entering the harbor of Port Royal, having made the voyage in less time than it had ever been made before. From the time we parted with our pilot off Sandy Hook, until we arrived at Jamaica, our wheels never stopped. By night and by day, whether we were sleeping or waking, whether watching or dreaming, the massive engine beneath us, like an imprisoned giant, with arms of iron and breath of flame, toiled on without fatigue and without repose. The weather was uniformly fine, and all the incidents of the voyage conspired to make it pleasant.

The interior accommodations of the Empire City are palatial. I enjoyed the exclusive use of a state-room, most eligibly situated with a sitting-room adjacent, luxuriously furnished. Our table abounded with all the luxuries of the New York market, dispensed by one of the most hospitable of captains, and our company was exceedingly pleasant, in spite of all the trying familiarities to which one is exposed in the cabins of populous ships.

Among our fellow passengers was Mr. Catherwood, the artist, who was on his way to Central America, whence, after a sojourn of a few months, he proposed to embark for California on a professional visit.   His large experience as a traveller in every quarter of the globe, rendered him an interesting and useful addition to our mess.

Gen. S. G. Taylor, cousin of the late President Zachary Taylor, was also of our company, accompanied by his wife, his son, Captain Marcellus K. Taylor and his wife, a poodle dog and a parrot.   General Taylor so closely resembles his distinguished cousin that I thought they were brothers before I was told that they were kindred.   He lacks the perceptive faculties which were the most prominent intellectual endowments of Zachary, but in other respects the likeness is very striking.   For some years past the General has been consul at Bogota.   I believe he holds the office still, though he is not attending to its duties if it have any.   He was now on his way to the Isthmus for the purpose of prosecuting a speculation in gold mining in which he was engaged, with some others, in that region. A disparity of some forty years between his own age and that of his wife seemed only to increase his devotion to her, and his consideration for the comforts of what seemed nearer to her than any other living things, except himself,

her parrot and her poodle, which he tended unremittingly
when her attention was, as it sometimes had to be, with-
drawn from one or both of them. Her devotion to these
pets were something of an annoyance to some of her fellow passengers, especially to a consumptive gentleman
from New York, who was bound to Jamaica in quest of
health, and who was the involuntary auditor of all the conversation which passed between them; but it proved at the
same time, that if Providence had permitted her marriage
with the General to be attended with the usual blessings
of matrimony, she would have made a most affectionate
and devoted mother.

Capt. Marcellus K. Taylor, the son of the General, by a
former marriage, attained some distinction in the Mexican
war for his bravery and professional resources. He had
the credit of having devised and constructed the corn-
stalk bridge across the ravine near Monterey, over which
his uncle, the President, marched his whole army in safety
to the attack of that place. He was, also, one of the es-
cort appointed to attend General Santa Anna when he
retired from Mexico, after his defeat and surrender. I
judged him to be about thirty years of age.

Besides these, we were accompanied by two gentlemen
from New York, and a company of men in their employ,
who were going to Jamaica to engage in mining for copper, which they think may be found on that island in

great abundance. They have already secured a long lease
of the lands, or mountains, rather, on which the mines lie,
and speak of their speedy and complete success with entire
confidence.

The first land we made after taking leave of the heights
of Neversink, was the point of Mayaguana, about 1,200
miles from New York. A dangerous coral reef, which
projects from the island, gives this point some consequence,
as it has been more fatal to navigators than any other, I
believe, among the West India Islands.

It is a striking illustration of the triumphs of modern
navigation, that Captain Wilson was able to calculate his
courses with such accuracy, for a distance of four hundred
leagues, as to come within half a mile of the point towards
which he laid the course of the ship, when he took his
last departure from Barnegat. We fortunately reached it
during daylight; had we arrived in the night, we should
have been compelled to lie-too till morning, the channel
is so narrow and tortuous. In passing it from the south,
the captain says, on his return voyage, he always keeps on by
night or day, for he is enabled to get a "departure," so
recently, from the headlands of St. Domingo, that in the
absence of all currents, he can navigate the passage without difficulty; but in coming from the north, owing to the
variety of currents which one encounters in the Atlantic,
it is impossible for the navigator to calculate his position

with such accuracy as to make the passage in the night safe. An error of half a mile in his reckoning might be fatal.

The thermometer stood at 80° as we rounded Mayaguana, and many of the passengers, like myself, were imprudent enough to throw off their flannel under clothing. Sad experience has since taught me, that flannels are no where of so much importance to the health, as in tropical climates.

At seven o'clock on the morning of the 10th, we were boarded by a pilot, as we entered Kingston harbor. He was a mulatto, intelligent looking, and about 25 years of age. He seemed rather overcome by the good luck which had befallen him in getting so big a ship. He soon, however, recovered his self-possession, gave his orders to the man at the wheel, and conducted us safely up in front of Port Royal.

Before the ship had fairly stopped, we were surrounded with boats filled with negroes, some dressed decently and some indecently, and some not at all. They all talked at once a language which they designed for English, but as it would have been unintelligible to me under the most favorable circumstances, of course, amid all this confusion, it was like the apostle's preaching to the Greeks—foolishness.

Some of the boats were filled with oranges, bananas,

and star apples and other fruits, which our passengers were
expected to purchase. The empty boats were waiting for
a fare. Such of our company as proposed to land at
Jamaica, including myself, soon made a selection from the
group, and debarked with our baggage with as little delay
as possible. Before we reached the shore, the steamer was
ploughing her way again across the bay, on her route to
Chagres.

We were compelled to stop at Port Royal, to have our
baggage inspected by the custom-house officers, before
going over to Kingston. The revenue officers were mostly
colored people. I saw but one white oarsman in any of
the revenue boats, and in that one, the coxswain was a
colored man.

When the ceremony of inspection was over, we re-dis-
tributed ourselves in our boats, and bore away for Kingston,
about six miles distant, on the opposite side of the bay.
We had four colored oarsmen, under the command of
Commodore Brooks, himself, a very black man, with very
white linen, whose broad pennant of red, with a white
ball, swung at the mast head, to indicate that he was senior
officer of the port. He told me that he received his commission from the admiral on the station, and that no other
boatmen were at liberty to raise the red flag, but himself.
I was amused at the style in which these pretensions were
asserted, and asked him what he would do if one were so

irreverent as to appropriate his color. He said he would go and pull it down, but added, that no one would dare to attempt such an outrage. I felt my capacity to realize the dignity of our commander gradually expand, and when he added, that he had several other boats plying between Kingston and Port Royal, I was awed.

Our boat was very well in its way, but the oars were a novelty. They consisted of two pieces. One a long pole the entire length of the oar, of uniform size from end to end. The other was a board in the shape of an ordinary oar blade, which was spliced to the pole in three places, with a cord "and nothing else." The oarsmen struck the water with the side of the blade to which the pole was attached, instead of the smooth side, out of respect to some principle of hydrodynamics, with which I was not familiar. Instead of tholepins, they used a rope, tied to the side of the boat, through which the oar was passed, and by which it was detained near, if not in its place, when used. The Commodore defended both these novelties with a force of logic which required nothing but a stupidity among his hearers, corresponding with his own, to render perfectly conclusive. He was about two hours getting us over to Kingston, a distance of about five miles. During the voyage I had leisure to contemplate the striking scenery which bounds the city we were approaching, in the rear. A high range of hills, rising gradually to mountains, surrounds it on all sides.   These hills are indented, apparently, by the centurial washing of running waters, until they look as if some astringent had been poured over them in their days of formation, and corrugated their surface into its present shape.   They were green, and as I afterwards discovered, were cultivated and inhabited to their very summits.

As we approached the shore, and the vegetation began to reveal itself, I realized, for the first time, that we were within the tropics.   We have hot weather at the north, and custom-house officers and negroes—weather as hot, custom-house officers as troublesome, and negroes as black as any I have yet encountered, but I had never before seen the cocoa-nut and the plaintain growing, as I did now. Here, in the depth of winter, orange trees were dropping their fruit, and the bananas were ready to be plucked ; the the lignumvitæ tree waved its luxuriant foliage, orna- mented with a delicate blossom of surpassing beauty ; and in the distance, our eyes were directed to the waving sugar fields of the Caymanos, and on the mountains, to the abandoned coffee estates, belonging to the bankrupt Duke of Buckingham.   I was most impatient to get on shore, that I might stray into the country and stare the wonders of tropical vegetation full in the face.

Notwithstanding my impatience, I was compelled to submit to many delays.   My largest trunk, which was handled by the coachman in New York without difficulty, engaged the devoted exertions of four negroes, in the effort to draw it from the boat, which they effected by in- stalments, after turning it over, as they did every article of luggage, several times, and trying it in various ways and from opposite sides, as if to see if they could not in some way get the advantage of it. They were two hours in transporting our luggage from the boats to our lodgings, not half a mile distant. And as the sun was nearly verticle the whole time, their delays were not a little trying to the tempers of the best of us.

CHAPTER II.

THERE are no first-class hotels in Kingston, and the best accommodations for travellers are to be found at boarding houses, of which there are two or three claiming precedence, which compare with the others, as warts compare with corns. They are all kept and served by colored people, who enjoy the princely prerogative which attaches only to indolent people and kings; entire immunity from all the penalties of lapsed time. They have no idea of doing anything within any specified period, and punctuality with them is a word, but not a thing. The house at which I stopped was inferior to no other in Jamaica, and was in many respects satisfactory. It was, however, quite impossible to have anything done within any appointed period. If breakfast was ordered at eight o'clock, it was sure not to be ready till ten. If dinner were ordered at three, we congratulated ourselves if we got it by five. The waiters, of which there was an abundance, had no idea of saving steps. They would carry every article to the table separately, and would spend an hour running up and down stairs with things which, with a little forethought, they might have transported at a single trip. Excellent fresh fish, good mutton, poor poultry, and of course fruit of un-equalled richness and inexhaustible varieties were common-ly served in English style; the rooms were spacious and pleasant, though scantily furnished. It may be interesting to some to know that for these accommodations I paid fourteen dollars a week.

My first impressions of Kingston were not favorable, and I had no occasion upon further acquaintance to change them. The city is well enough situated, on ground gradu-ally rising from the sea, at the rate of about one hundred feet to the mile, and the mountains which bound it in the rear, about four miles distant, furnish a most desirable re-fuge from the extreme heats of summer, or to invalids who require a more bracing temperature occasionally than can be furnished below. In a drive of four hours, one may be transferred from an average temperature of eighty degrees to one of sixty. But the city of Kingston is a most undesi-rable residence. The streets are all quite narrow, scarcely wide enough for alleys. The houses are all partially dila-pidated, and of course old. Though I have been through nearly every street, I have not seen a single new house erecting, save an Insane Asylum, which, by the way, has been suspended for want of funds. A terrible fire laid a large portion of the city in ruins, several years ago, and only a portion of the houses have been rebuilt. These are commonly one story high only and very mean. In the busiest parts of the city, and on every block, may be seen vacant lots, on which are crumbling the foundation walls of houses long in ruins. Rents are exceedingly low, less than half a fair interest on the cost of the buildings alone—while the vacant lots cannot be said to have any market value, there being no sales. There are several fine houses yet extant here, but they were all built many years ago, when the island was prosperous, and very few of them are " in repair."

There is not a foot of street pavement to my knowledge, in Kingston, and the streets are almost uniformly from one to three feet lower in the centre than at the sides. This is the result of spring rains which wash down the mountains in torrents, and through the streets of the city to the river, oftentimes making such channels in them as to render them impassable. This periodical visitation was suggested to me by a resident, as the reason for not paving the street walks. That may be a good reason for Jamaica people, but it would not be a sufficient one for Yankees, if they had to use the streets. They would either remove the mountains altogether, or make such terms with the rains as would induce them to use the highways to the ocean, as not abusing them.

Kingston contains about forty thousand inhabitants at present, nine-tenths of whom, at least, are colored. In walking the streets, one scarcely meets white persons as frequently as he would meet colored persons in New York city. The whites are mostly English, or of English descent. The proportion of Jews of all colors is fearfully great. I had never seen a black Jew before, and I was, astonished to find how little the expression of the Israelitish profile was effected by color. My imagination could never have combined the sharp and cunning features of Isaac with the thick lipped, careless, unthinking countenance of Cudjo ; but nature has done it perfectly, if that can be called a combination in which the negro furnishes the color and the Jew all the rest of the expression. What will be the ultimate consequence of this corruption of the African blood, is a question over which the wise men of Jamaica are already beginning to scratch their heads.

Though Kingston is the principal port of the island, it has but little of the air of a commercial city. One looks and listens in vain for the noise of carts and the bustle of busy men ; no one seems to be in a hurry, but few are doing anything, while the mass of the population are lounging about in idleness and rags. The business is mostly mercantile, and confined to three or four streets. Here are no mechanics or mechanical operatives such as abound in the larger cities of the north. Nearly all who do not

traffic, wait upon those who do, or lead a life of comparative indolence.   The professional men are about the only
exceptions.

The white inhabitants are almost all of British descent.
It is an uncommon thing to meet a Frenchman or a Spa-
niard in Kingston.   The English language is universally
spoken, and in every variety of African dialect.   They
have what they call the omnibus here, which is of the capacity and shape of a four-wheeled cab.   These vehicles
pursue no specific route, but carry their passengers to any
part of the city for twenty-five cents, provided their starved
horses are equal to the effort.   I never tried any of them
but twice, but on both those occasions the horses gave out
more than once before they reached my place of destination.

I never saw a place so abounding in old people and
babies.   Almost every woman you meet, and of whatever
age, has an infant in her arms or somewhere upon her person, while the streets are littered with children more advanced.   So aged persons are far more abundant here than
in our northern cities.   This may be attributed to the
mildness of the weather, which enables the old people to
be in the streets at all seasons, without exposing them to
those infirmities with which our northern climates afflict
the aged.   But the fact probably is, that while in the north
the poor aged people die of neglect, privation and exposure,
as soon as they become too infirm to provide for all the

wants occasioned by our trying climate and long cold winters, in Jamaica the same class do not reach any such crisis, until much more advanced in years. They never feel cold weather, they can easily get all they require for their support if they can walk, so abundant are the fruits and edible productions of the island ; and though the ties which bind the parent and child together are generally much more frail here than at the north, and though the aged rarely depend upon their children for any assistance, yet the means of subsistence are so much more accessible, that one never hears of a person contracting disease or suffering very seriously for want of food.

I here beheld, for the first time, a class of beings of whom we have heard much, and for whom I have felt considerable interest. I refer to the Coolies, imported by the British government to take the place of the *faineant* negroes, when the apprenticeship system was abolished. Those that I saw were wandering about the streets, dressed rather tastefully, but always meanly, and usually carrying over their shoulder a sort of *chiffionier's* sack, in which they threw whatever refuse stuff they found in the streets, or received as charity. Their figures are generally superb, and their eastern costume, to which they adhere as far as their poverty will permit of any clothing, sets off their lithe and graceful forms to great advantage. Their faces are almost uniformly of the finest classic mould, and illuminated by pairs of those dark swimming and propitiatory eyes, which exhaust the language of tenderness and passion at a glance.

But they are the most inveterate mendicants on the island. It is said that those brought from the interior of India are faithful and efficient workmen, while those from Calcutta and its vicinity are good for nothing. Those that were prowling about the streets of Spanishtown and Kingston, I presume, were of the latter class, for there is not a planter on the island it is said, from whom it would be more difficult to get any work than from one of these. They subsist by begging altogether, they are not vicious, nor intemperate, nor troublesome particularly, except as beggars. In that calling they have a pertinacity before which a northern mendicant would grow pale. They will not be denied. They will stand perfectly still and look through a window from the street for a quarter of an hour if not driven away, with their imploring eyes fixed upon you, like a stricken deer, without saying a word, or moving a muscle. They act as if it were no disgrace for them to beg, as if the least indemnification which they are entitled to expect, for the outrage perpetrated upon them in bringing them from their distant homes to this strange island, is a daily supply of their few and cheap necessities, as they call for them.

I confess that their begging did not leave upon my mind the impression produced by ordinary mendicancy. They do not look as if they ought to work. I never saw one smile, and though they showed no positive suffering, I never saw one look happy. Each face seemed to be constantly telling the unhappy story of their woes, and like fragments of a broken mirror, each reflecting in all its hateful proportions the national outrage of which they are the victims.

CHAPTER III.

Intermarriage between the whites and browns—Public sentiment about color—The proportion of colored and white people in public and professional employments—Colored people of note —The English policy towards them.

It was sixteen years in August, since slavery was abolished on this island, and the apprenticeship system, which took its place, was abolished four years later. Since that period, the laws have recognised no complexional distinctions among the inhabitants. The black people have enjoyed the same political privileges as the whites, and with them have shared the honors and the patronage of the mother and local governments.

The effect of this policy upon the people of color may be partially anticipated ; but one accustomed to the proscribed condition of the free blacks in the United States, will constantly be startled at the diminished importance attached here to the matter of complexion. Intermarriages are constantly occurring between the white and colored people, their families associate together within the ranks to which by wealth and culture they respectively belong, and public opinion does not recognise any social distinctions based exclusively upon color. Of course, cultivated or fashionable people will not receive colored persons of inferior culture and worldly resources, but the rule of discrimination is scarcely more rigorous against those than against whites. They are received at the "King's House"—it is thus the Governor's residence is styled—and they are invited to his table with fastidious courtesy. The wife of the present Mayor of Kingston is a "brown" woman—that is the name given to all the intermediate shades between a decided white and decided black complexion—so also is the wife of the Receiver General himself, an English gentleman, and one of the most exalted public functionaries upon the island.

A circumstance occurred shortly after I arrived, which may be interesting to some in this connection. It was proposed by some of the officers stationed near Kingston, and gentlemen resident in and about the city, to give a public ball. They proceeded to engage the theatre for the occasion. Some Jews who, as a class, incline to indemnify themselves for their exclusion from the society of the whites by striking an alliance with the people of color, circulated among the latter a report that the committee on invitations to the ball had resolved, that "no colored person, Jew or Dog," should be invited. Of course the story produced considerable excitement among those most concerned.

The theatre belongs to the city. The committee " on
the theatre" in the Common Council, composed of a majority of brown men, quietly turned the key of the theatre,
and excluded the artizans sent to arrange it for the festival.
The ball had to be postponed in consequence, and finally
took place at the Camp, a much more desirable place in
every particular.   I was assured by members of the ball
committee, that the Jew's report was false altogether—
that they had resolved upon no such exclusions.   They
did not propose to invite Jews, because no social intercourse had existed between them and their respective
families, nor did it appear that either party desired
any; but they said that invitations had been sent to the
daughters of the Receiver General and of the Mayor;
—all, as I have before mentioned, browns.   Before the
ball took place, I believe the colored people became satisfied that they had been deceived, for a brown gentleman
spoke to me with some bitterness, of a determination formed
by the committee on invitations, as he professed to know
of his own knowledge, to invite to the ball no persons who
had ever been behind a counter ; but he made no allusion
to the other report.

One unacquainted with the extent to which the amalga-
mation of races has gone here, is constantly liable to drop
remarks in the presence of white persons, which, in consequence of the mixture of blood that may take place in

some branch of their families, are likely to be very offensive. I was only protected from frequent *contretemps* of
this kind, by the timely caution of a lady, who, in explain-
ing its propriety, said that unless one knows the whole col-
lateral kindred of a family in Jamaica, he is not safe in
assuming that they have not some colored connections.

One of the most distinguished barristers on the island is
a colored man, who was educated at an English university,
and ate his terms at Lincoln's inn, as must all barristers
who wish to practice here ; the judicial authorities of the
island having no power to admit any one to practice the
law in any of its departments. This is a circumstance, by
the way, which has given to Jamaica a bar of no inconsiderable culture and talent.

It so happened that the Surry Assize was sitting in
Kingston when I arrived, Sir Joshua Rowe presiding. I
availed myself of the courtesy of a professional friend, and
accompanied him one day to the court, while in session.
Though the room contained a crowd of people, there did
not appear to be twenty white persons among them, the
court and bar inclusive. Two colored lawyers were sitting
at the barrister's table, and the jury box was occupied by
twelve men, all but three of whom were colored, and all
but two who were negroes, were Jews. Two witnesses
were examined before I left the room, both of whom were
colored and both police officers. All the officers of the

court, except the clerk, were also colored. I was assured that more than seven-tenths of the whole police force of the island, amounting to about eight hundred men, are colored. Judging from the proportion that fell under my observation, this estimate cannot be far from correct. I may as well add here, that in the Legislative Assembly of Jamaica, composed of from forty-eight to fifty British subjects, some ten or a dozen are colored men. Nay, more, the public printers of the legislature, Messrs. Jordon & Osborn, are both colored men, and are likewise editors of the leading government paper, the Kingston Journal.

It was my privilege, shortly after my arrival, to make the acquaintance of one of the most highly cultivated men I ever met, upon whose complexion the accidents of birth had left a tinge which betrayed the African bar on his escutcheon. I refer to Mr. Richard Hill, of Spanishtown. He is a brown man, about forty-five years of age, I judged, and was educated in one of the English universities, where he enjoyed every advantage which wealth could procure for his improvement. His appearance and address both indicate superior refinement. He enjoys an enviable reputation as a naturalist, and has published a volume on the birds of Jamaica, illustrated by his own pencil, which displays both literary and scientific merit of a high order. He is one of the stipendiary magistrates of the island, upon a salary of £500 sterling per annum.

It is the policy of the present administration, both in Downing street and Spanishtown, to promote intercourse in every possible way, between the different races in Jamaica, and throughout the British West India Islands; and, to this end, the colored people are familiarized as rapidly as possible with the political duties of the citizen—as John Bull understands them. They have, certainly, a fair share of the public patronage, indeed they are esteemed the favorites of the government; there are one or two black regiments here constantly under pay; they furnish nine-tenths of the officers of the penitentiary, and, as I have before said, almost the entire police force of the island, and ultimately, I have reason to believe, it is the expectation of the home government, that these islands, without changing their colonial relations, will be substantially abandoned by the white population, and their local interests left to the exclusive management of the people of color. But more of this anon.

While the *entente cordiale* between the whites and the colored people is apparently strengthening, daily, a very different state of feeling exists between the negroes or Africans, and the browns. The latter shun all connection by marriage with the former, and can experience no more unpardonable insult, than to be classified with them in any way. They generally prefer that their daughters should live with a white person upon any terms, than be married to

a negro.   Few will need to be told that where such is the
condition of public sentiment in a class, the standard of
female virtue among them cannot be very high.   It is,
perhaps, a trifle higher than among the slaves.*

It is their ambition that their offspring should be light
complexioned, and there are few sacrifices they will not
make to accomplish that result, whether married or not.
Color with them, in a measure, marks rank, and they have

---

* Lest I should be supposed from these remarks, to countenance an opinion
quite popular in some quarters, that licentiousness is an inherent vice in the negro
character, I may as well state, that the training received by the black population
during the prevalence of slavery, is more than sufficient to account for any kind of
intimacy between the sexes which is found to exist here, unless, perhaps, it should
be one of a virtuous character.   The masters would rarely permit, and almost
uniformly discouraged matrimony among the slaves, for reasons sufficiently obvious to those who can bring themselves to look for a moment upon human bond-
men in an exclusively financial point of view.   The same selfishness tended to
discourage matrimony among the overseers and agents, and often the loss of their
situation was the penalty which they paid for presuming to rear children for their
own honor rather than of slaves for the profit of their employers.   In a recent
sketch of a trip to Jamaica, made by the Rev. Dr. King, I found some facts stated
as coming within his observation which confirmed what I have said.   He says :—

" A missionary, in whose word I can thoroughly confide, informed me that four
negroes, who had attended for some time on his instructions, intimated to him their
earnest desire to marry the women with whom they were living in concubinage,
and expressed to him their hope that he would intercede for them with their masters to have the measure sanctioned.   He wrote a respectful letter to the proper
authorities, soliciting their acquiescence, and despatched it to its destination on a
Saturday forenoon.   No notice of the communication was taken till Monday, when
the four negroes were called out, stripped, and lashed, and then told to show their
bleeding backs to their parson, and acquaint him that this was the answer to his
letter !   The prohibition against marriage extended to whites as well as to blacks.
A book-keeper or overseer perilled his situation by marrying without the consent
of the attorney or proprietor ; and usually it was vain to solicit any such concurrence.   To the present day difficulties are occasionally interposed by the same
parties to the formation of the nuptial union ; and I was requested, in one case, to
use my influence in obviating this kind of opposition.   An attorney agreed to
wave further resistance to his book-keeper's wedding, on the whimsical condition
that I should accomplish a considerable journey to perform the marriage ceremony.
When such was the state of the whole colony, when fornication and adultery
were everywhere practised by the lords of the soil, and the imperious agents of
their pleasure, who could expect the seventh commandment to be regarded by
the negro, or what could be looked for from systematic and penal suppression of
its observance but the desertion of females, the neglect of progeny, and the
general dissolution of morals by which Jamaica is now afflicted ?"

the same fear of being confounded with what they deem
an inferior caste, that is so often exhibited by vulgar people, who have no ascertained or fixed social position.

It was in consequence of the state of feeling, which I
have described, that Soulouque, the Emperor of Hayti, who
is utterly black, is stated to have recently commenced his
terrible system of persecution against the browns. Upon
the pretence that they were conspiring against his government, or contemplated other capital offences, he issued
warrants for the arrest of all the prominent brown men
within his Empire. They were obliged to abscond preci-
pitately, to save their lives. Many of them took refuge in
Jamaica.

I visited one who cultivates a small plantation of about
twenty acres, near Kingston. Nothing about him but his
complexion and his hair indicated African blood. He had
a fine intelligent countenance, and good address. His
grounds were under admirable culture, and displayed skill,
industry and thrift. His tobacco beds were his pride, but
around them the rarest tropical fruits and vegetables to be
found upon the island, were growing in luxuriant perfection. He had been stripped of most of his property by
the Emperor, but he was living here in apparent comfort
and respectability. Upon the walls of the room in which
my companion and myself were shown, were suspended
two portraits, one of his wife and the other of his daughter,

who, he informed me, is now in Paris, at school. If the likeness be correct, the original must be exceedingly beautiful. The paintings were both of superior merit as works of art.

His wife had not been permitted by the Emperor to join him, nor did he enjoy very frequent opportunities of hearing from her. He alluded to his domestic sorrows with great feeling, but with a Frenchman's hopefulness, he looked for a time when justice should be done.

Of course his indignation against Soulouque was very strong, nor was he much disposed to extenuate his majesty's faults; and yet a brief conversation with him first led me to doubt whether the Emperor, any more than the devil, was half as black as he had been painted. I afterwards satisfied myself that he was not. From what I heard and saw I concluded that he administered a strong central government with as much gentleness as would consist with the greatest good of the greatest number. He is, doubtless, a more beneficent ruler than any brown man would have been, because, in the first place, he belongs to much the more numerous caste, there being many more blacks than browns on the island. In the next place the browns are very generally cunning and false, they are oppressive upon the blacks when they have power, and are universally more indisposed than the blacks to any productive labor. It seems better, therefore, that the blacks should have a representative of their own than of a lighter class, unless he be absolutely white, to govern them; and from all I can learn, a better man than Soulouque was not easily to be found. He is a man of strong will, unsurpassed courage, an accomplished soldier, knows the people he rules perfectly, and in spite of all the scoffers of black government may say to the contrary, is kindly disposed to his people, and to all but his enemies. During my stay in Jamaica a French gentleman who was inquiring into the condition of the negro population of the West India islands, passed a month on the island of Hayti. After his return, he wrote an account of his visit to the court of the Haytien Emperor, in the form of a letter, which was dated at Kingston, March 18, 1850. This visit was so recent, the account of it is so unprejudiced and satisfactory, it bears so directly upon matters to which I am chiefly desirous of directing the attention of my readers, and withal it is likely to reach so few of them in any other way, that I feel that I shall add materially to whatever of interest or value these pages may possess, by publishing the communication entire. It will be found in the Appendix A.

CHAPTER IV.

Spanishtown—Governor Grey—His embarrassments—His family
—House of Assembly—The Public Printers—The Speaker—
His compensation.

St. Jago de la Vega, now and for more than a hundred
years past called Spanishtown by the people, is the political centre of the island. It lies about east of Kingston,
and is reached by traversing twelve out of the only fourteen
miles of railroad in Jamaica. The inhabitants do nothing
here in a hurry, and it is not surprising therefore, that the
average time made by the trains between the two cities, is
not less than forty-five minutes, or fifteen miles the hour,
for which passengers are expected to pay the sum of
seventy-five cents. Slow as it is, however, it is the only
punctual thing upon the island. I was told, in this respect, that it was working an important revolution in the
habits of the islanders. The road had been in operation
several months before any body believed it was in earnest
in its hours of departure, and no one ever reached the
train desired in season. They have since learned that
the habits of the locomotive are inflexible, and no one now

presumes to expect from it the same indulgence to their laziness which is safely reckoned upon, from every other style of conveyance.

Spanishtown is one of the oldest places on this continent. It is supposed to have been founded by Diego Columbus, the brother of the discoverer, in 1523. No one visiting the place at this time, will dispute its antiquity, nor experience much difficulty in believing that all the houses at present standing, were built before Diego left the island, so old and ruinous is their general appearance.

The Governor's residence is here ; here the Parliament holds its session uniformly, and the superior courts occasionally ; and here are the government offices and public records. The occupants of these public buildings and the persons employed about them, represent the wealth, intelligence and industry of the city. I did not see a store in the place, though there may have been one or two perhaps ; it has not a single respectable hotel, nor did I see a dray-cart, or any similar evidence of activity and thrift, although a population of 5,000 people is said to be lodged within its precincts. The city is supported mainly out of the public treasury. Those that have anything are generally connected in some way, directly or indirectly, with the public service, and those that have not anything, wait upon those who have.

The public buildings form a quadrangle, one side of

which is the " King's House,"—the residence of the Governor—opposite to it is the Parliament House and the other
two sides are devoted to the public offices and courts.
This is all of Spanishtown worthy of notice.

The present Governor of the island is Sir Charles E.
Grey, a cousin of Earl Grey, Her Britannic Majesty's
Secretary for the Colonies. He is about sixty years of age
I should judge, and rather stout but vigorous and active.
He is far from being handsome but nature has endowed
him with a benevolent disposition, a rare and genial hu-
mor, and more than ordinary executive talents, which, with
the aid of high culture and rare experience, have made
him a decidedly noticeable man. He was educated to the
bar, and practised in the courts of Westminster Hall for
some years, not without distinction. During my visit in
Spanishtown, the British steamer Teviot arrived, bringing
the young Earl of Durham, yet quite a lad, who, for the
sake of his health, had chosen this, instead of the more
direct route, to visit his sister, Lady Elgin, in Canada.
His arrival furnished the Governor an occasion for mentioning that the first fee he ever received as a barrister, was
two hundred and fifty guineas from this lad's father, in the
case of his contested election to a seat in Parliament, many
years ago. The result of the contest vindicated Lord
Durham's sagacity, and at once gave the young barrister
professional position.

His family connection and serviceable talents transferred him, at a comparitively early age, from the bar to the highly important post of judge in India, where he presided with distinction for many years. He was subsequently appointed Governor of the island of Barbadoes, from whence he was promoted to his present position, which is esteemed the second governorship, in point of dignity, in the gift of the crown—Canada being the first. One of the Governor's friends here told me, that if Lord Elgin should retire from Canada, Sir Charles would unquestionably be appointed to his place. The change I think would be popular in Canada, though one of the prominent reasons for removing Elgin, would constitute a fatal objection to appointing Sir Charles as his successor. Both are necessitous, and cannot spare any portion of their incomes to popularize and strengthen themselves with among their people ; Elgin does not scruple to use the £300 appropriated to him by his government for entertaining, to the paying off of incumbrances upon his estates, and in consequence enjoys the reputation of being a screw and a niggard throughout Canada. Sir Charles Grey is deeply in debt, and I believe has been outlawed by his creditors ; at all events, his embarrassments were such that he was obliged to leave England. He has been repeatedly prosecuted in the courts of the island for his liabilities, and recently had the hardihood to plead his governorship in bar of an action upon one of his bonds.   The courts very properly decided that governors have no "privilege" which exempted them from the payment of their debts, and he was compelled to pay.   Thus pressed at all times by his creditors, of course he never has a spare penny which is not required to satisfy them, and has no means to entertain them with that liberality which his taste would incline him, and which made Lord Metcalf so exceedingly popular both in Jamaica and afterwards in Canada.

Lady Grey resides with her daughters, in England.   Lieut. Charles William, the son of the Governor, is with him in the capacity of assistant secretary.   This separation of the family, I am told, is one of the consequences of the father's improvidence and pecuniary necessities.   The catastrophe, however, is so enveloped in scandal that I do not feel authorized upon my information to give its details farther currency.

The Governor is *ex officio* Chancellor, the presiding officer of the "Court of Ordinary," and presiding officer of the "Court of Appeals under Errors."   He is also vested with the powers of a High Court of Admiralty.   As Governor, he receives a salary of $30,000 a year, which is increased by the fees accruing from his various judicial offices some eight or ten thousand more.   His official income is not over estimated at forty thousand dollars an-

nually ; a very pretty sum for a plain man, but not much
for a nobleman, they say.

Opposite to the Governor's residence, is the House of
Assembly or Parliament House, where I was impatient to
meet the assembled legislative wisdom of the island, and
whither I bent my steps as soon after my arrival as circumstances would permit.

When I entered, the House was " in Committee of th
Whole on the State of the Island," Mr. Jordan, a brow ̗
man, and one of the editors of the Morning Journal, in
the chair.   Mr. Osborne, another brown man, his associate
in the editorship of the Journal, was speaking.   About
twenty-five members were present.   The room was a plain,
indeed homely sort of an apartment, competent to hold
three or four hundred people, and divided in two by a bar,
within which sat the members.   The room was entirely
without ornament of any kind, and resembled a country
court room in the United States.   Mr. Jordan, who occupied the chair, is a clear headed, deliberate, and sagacious
man, and is perhaps as much as any one, the leader of
what is called the King's House or administration party.

Osborne, who was speaking when I entered, was originally a slave ; I afterwards had occasion to observe that he
talked more than any other man in the house, though I
did not perceive that he had any particular vocation as an
orator.   He is not educated ; he is, however, rather illiter-

ate than ignorant, and his mind lacks discipline and order, but he has an influence with his colleagues which is not to be despised. He is sanguine and pertinacious to a degree, and by taking advantage of the heedlessness or indolence of his colleagues, accomplishes more than many members of superior capacity. He and Jordan are the public printers, from which appointment they derive a profit which is supposed here to exceed thirty thousand dollars a year. It is not surprising, therefore, that in the Assembly and in their journal they support the present administration fervently.

The Speaker, Charles M'Larty Morales, is of Jewish descent, and by profession a physician. He contested his present seat successfully with Samuel Jackson Dallas, the previous incumbent, who I learned to my surprise, is a cousin to the late Vice President of the United States. Mr. Dallas represents Port Royal; he is very tall, quite thin, and grey, and looks like a gentleman, but shares few of the advantages of personal appearance which distinguish his American cousin.

The Speaker is chosen by the Assembly, subject to the matter-of-course approval of the Governor. He is the only member who receives any compensation. As Speaker he is allowed £960 per annum, nearly $5,000; at least that was the sum allowed to Mr. Dallas, by a law passed in 1845, and I think no change has been made in that salary since. I am the more confident of this, from a circumstance which occurred during my visit on the island. Some of the friends of Morales brought forward a proposition to advance the Speaker's salary, when a member rose and with crushing effect, produced the journal of the House of some previous year, in which Morales's vote was recorded against the law which advanced the Speaker's salary to its present figure, upon the ground that the old salary was high enough. Of course the proposition met with no favor.

Had I realized what a set of shadows composed this body, and how utterly destitute they were of the independence and the power which give to political representation all its value, I should have felt less impatience to visit it. I had expected to find there, as in the United States and as in England, the troubles of the people finding fit expression. I supposed the reports, debates and legislative formula's would have revealed the activity, the tendencies, the grievances, and in general the public sentiment of Jamaica; instead of which, I found a body of men in no respect representatives of the people, holding legislative office without the vital functions of legislators.

CHAPTER V.

I HAVE stated that the local legislature of this island has
neither the independence nor the power necessary to make
it, to any extent, representative of the people.   A few facts
will show the truth of what I say, and will go far to explain the decrepit condition of this colony, to those who
appreciate the dependance of good government upon full
and fair representation.

Jamaica is divided up into twenty-two parishes, as they
are called, each of which sends two, and Kingston, Spanishtown and Port Royal, one additional delegate to the
assembly, making the aggregate forty-seven, when the
house is full.   Every member, before taking his seat, is
required to swear that he and his wife together, if he have
a wife, are in the receipt of a clear income of nine hundred
dollars a year, from real estate, or that they own real
estate worth nine thousand dollars, or real and personal

estate together, worth about fifteen thousand dollars ; and when he gets his seat he is obliged to discharge its duties without any compensation.

A high property qualification like this, of course reduces the number of persons eligible to the assembly to a very small figure, and throws the legislation, not only into the hands of the comparatively rich, but into the hands of the landholders. The poor are utterly excluded from all participation in its privileges or responsibilities.

Such discriminations are as pernicious as they are absurd, and have resulted, as any statesman could have anticipated, indeed, as they were probably designed to result, in subordinating the interest of the commercial, mechanical and industrial classes to that of the large landholders. All the energies of legislation are exerted to promote the growth and sale of sugar and rum ; but there is no party in the assembly inquiring about the inexhaustible commercial and manufacturing resources of the island.

In spite of these conditions, imposed by law upon candidates applying for seats in the legislature, they might still possess some of the more important representative functions if their constituency were free, and if the right of suffrage were liberally extended. But here again we find a characteristic distrust of poor men, and a truly English anxiety to guard the landholder. Every voter must own a freehold estate worth thirty dollars, or pay a yearly rent on real estate of not less than one hundred and forty dollars, or pay yearly taxes to the amount of fifteen dollars. The first consequence of these restrictions is, that the *people* of the island are not only ineligible to the legislature, but they have nothing to do with making a selection from those who are. I say people, for of course the great bulk of the adult population are poor ; they are colored people who, only sixteen years ago, were, with no considerable exception, slaves. Of the 400,000 people who, according to the received estimate, constitute the present population of Jamaica, but 16,000 are white. The remaining 384,000 are colored and black people. The last census taken upon the island fixed the proportion of these as follows : colored, 68,529 ; blacks, 293,128.* The average vote of this en-

---

* A census of the island was taken on the third day of June, 1844, and the following results were obtained :

	Males.	Females.	Total.
White,	9,289	6,4·7	15,776
Colored,	31,646	36,883	68,529
Black,	140,693	452 430	293,128
Totals,	181,633	195,890	877,433

The ages of the population were thus classified :

	Males.	Females.	Sex not specified.	Total.
Under 5 years	20,575	22,884	8,248	31,707
Between 5 and 10	18,472	21,534	7,215	47,221
Between 10 and 20	25,916	27,432	9,385	62,733
Between 20 and 40	50.834	50,919	20,006	121 309
Between 40 and 60	27,896	29,532	11,069	68,499
Over 60	9,576	12,628	3,759	25,963
Total				877,433

By the above tables, it appears, that every thousand inhabitants are, according to color, in the following proportion : White, 41 '79 ; Colored, 181 '56 ; Black, 776 '63.

The proportion of females to every 100 males is 107 '79 ; according to color for every one hundred white males, there are 69 '83 white females ; for every 100 colored males, 110 '22 colored females ; and for every 100 black males, 108 '33 black females.

tire population, white and black, I understand, has never
exceeded three thousand—or, three quarters per cent.
The city of New York, with about the same population,
usually polls over fifty thousand votes, which is a smaller
proportion probably, than is polled in any other county in
any free state of the Union.

But this is not all. When the legislature is chosen, it
has no control over the questions of fundamental interest.
The heart which gives it life, beats in London; the islanders
have no more control over its action than the finger nails
have over the circulation of the blood. The Assembly, in
connexion with the Executive and Council, can levy taxes
for local purposes, it must raise money to pay the officers
sent out to rule over it; it can keep the highways in condition, it must support the established church; it may provide
public instruction, it may establish a police; but even these
powers it exercises subject to the approval of the Queen or
of Parliament. The organization of their local government, the appointments to fill the various executive offices,
and the taxes payable upon imports and exports, are all
matters with which the island legislature has nothing to
do. But even in its local legislature I have not exhibited
all its impotence.

The Governor is vested with power " to adjourn, pro-
rogue, or *dissolve*" the Assembly at his pleasure, and is
invested with almost the entire patronage of the island,

which is altogether controlling. Some notion of its extent may be formed from the following items, which have fallen under my observation. He appoints the Vice-Chancellor, with a salary of about $12,500 a year; two assistant Judges, with salaries of $10,000 a year each; six chairmen of quarter sessions, at $6,000 a year each; three revising barristers to canvass the votes of the island annually, at $1,000 a year each; a commissioner of stamps, at $2,500 a year; three official assignees of insolvents, at $2,500 a year each; nine water bailiffs to regulate the landing and discharge of vessels, with salaries at discretion; seventeen health officers and an indefinite number of assistants, at undefined salaries; an agent general of immigration, at a salary of $1,500 a year; an inspector general of police, at a discretionary compensation; an inspector general of prisons, at a salary of $3,000 a year; a superintendent at $1,500; an auditor of accounts at $2,000; and some fifty subordinate officers; and finally, he has the extraordinary power of suspending any member of the Council, and of appointing a new member in his place.

I have not alluded before to the Second Estate of the island, the Council, which, as a nominal branch of the local government, is worthy of some notice.

The Council is the upper house of legislation in Jamaica, and is composed of twelve men appointed by the crown, of whom the Lieutenant Governor, the Chief Justice, the Attorney General and the Bishop, are *ex-officio* members. All bills originate with the lower house, but they must pass the Council before they go to the Executive or can become laws. Of course, nothing can pass this body, thus constituted and appointed, which is not perfectly satisfactory to the Colonial minister, nor does anything ever pass it against the wishes of the Governor. It is nominally a branch of the legislature, but in fact is nothing but a cabinet or sort of privy counsel, with which the Governor consults, and which he uses as a sort of breakwater between himself and the lower house. They are an independent legislative body upon questions in which the Governor has no adverse interest, but they are as incapable of making any resistance to his will as his shadow would be.*

* During my stay in Jamaica, an information, was filed by the Attorney General against William Girod, the editor of the Colonial Standard, the organ of the country party, for a libel upon the Council. It seems that the Council had received a petition, signed by some members of Assemby, among others, imputing corrupt motives to a portion of that body in their legislative proceedings Girod was a member of the Assembly, and belonged to the party which this petition assailed. He denounced the Council for receiving it, and, among other things said :

We are not skilled enough in parliamentary law, to be able to state the extent to which the Council have sinned against that degree of etiquette, which custom at least, if not mutual respect, has ever maintained between the two lower branches of the legislature. But this we know, that the Council have now opened the door to recrimination, and they need not be surprised, if at an early opportunity, the true opinion of the people of Jamaica, of those who are competent to offer an opinion, the wealth, the education and the respectability of the country, finds its way in the form of accumulated contempt of the Council, their selfishness, their corruption and their avarice, upon the journals of the Assembly.

For this he was prosecuted by the government. He was successfully defended by Mr. Moncrieff, who, by the by, is a brown man, and one of the most eloquent advocates in Jamaica. The following extract from his speech, will be found to confirm the view I have taken of its operation as a branch of the government :

"Now, let me ask, if these opinions expressed in this publication before you, are the opinions of yesterday ?—if they are noxious to society ?—if the object was to subvert society, or if the object of William Girod was to sow sedition in the minds of the inhabitants of this country ? Gentlemen, as matter of history,

From the illustrations here presented, it is apparent that the executive patronage reaches every point of influence and every interest worth conciliating or promoting on the island, and enables the Governor practically to dictate its legislation. It is hardly necessary to say that the deliberations of a body thus constituted and crippled, possess but little interest to strangers, and furnish a very narrow theatre for the display of oratory or statesmanship. The questions never involve any principle, and the discussions

these opinions are not of yesterday. In 1792, it was the opinion of those who then represented the people of the colony, 'That it be recommended to the House to appoint a committee to prepare an humble address to his majesty, grounded on the several preceding resolutions, and humbly to represent to his majesty, that the junction of two such different capacities as that of a privy council of State and a legislative council, in one and the same body, of which five members only constitute a quorum, (no greater number having attended the Board during the late contest,) has ever been productive of great inconvenience to the good people of this island. and has proved, and must always prove, the never-failing source of discord and distrust between this House and the King's representative, (and the time now gives it proof;) and lastly, to pray his majesty graciously to afford such relief in the premises, as to his royal wisdom shall seem meet. Ordered, That Mr. Bryan Edwards, Mr. W. Mitchell and Mr. Shirley, be a committee for that purpose.' (Journals of Assembly, Vol. 9, page 100) Gentlemen, in 1812, those who then represented the public opinion of the colony resolved, 'That the Council of this island, as at present constituted, have not necessarily a territorial qualification in the country, or any community of interest with the inhabitants, to whom they are in no manner accountable, that nothing can more clearly prove the danger of such a body having any control over the property of our constituents, than the late wanton rejection of a law necessary to the public safety, because the House would not surrender its most important privileges.' So far back, then, as 1792, the bold men who represented the colonists predicted, and predicted truly, that so long as an oligarchy existed in this colony, so long as there existed an irresponsible body having legislative power over the people of this country—so long as that anomalous Board existed, there would be no peace in the colony; and with the opinions so long ago uttered, I, from what has taken place within the last few years, cordially agree; and I say that for a body of that description to proscribe any other than their opinions to punish us for uttering opinions other than theirs, will never meet with the concurrence of a jury, or there would not be one single moment's security for any of us. It is for this reason, gentlemen, that I ask you if you are to convict William Girod of libel, for uttering opinions which have prevailed now for more than half a century? For uttering the opinions of a large body of the inhabitants of this country? Whether public opinion shall be crushed and stifled by a body exercising tyrannical power? I say, gentlemen, and I say it advisedly, that where irresponsible power decides there is tyranny; human passion will make tyrants of an oligarchy, and this prosecution shows what that Board would do if you would assist them; they would cramp the expression of opinion; they would circumscribe our opinions to their own limits; they would do what despotic power always does, they would ride rampant over the people."

are never elaborate. Though the assembly contains many gentlemen of talent and prominence in their respective callings, they never find occasion to display it here. Their debates are quite as informal and colloquial as those of the New York Municipal Council, and their legislation disposes of far less considerable interests in the course of a year.

It is difficult to convey any satisfactory idea of the state of political parties here, for they can hardly be said to have any state. They are not arrayed upon any of the issues which classify the inhabitants of the mother country. Upon the questions agitated in the British parliament in which they have any interest, they are for the most part agreed. Colonial assistance of any kind all desire, and all desire protection for colonial produce. The appointees of the present government have prudence enough not to pro-claim their sentiments upon the house-tops, but even they, do not disguise them at the fire-side. It is to free trade they ascribe their ruin, not to the abolition of slavery. I did not find a man upon the island, and I made very extensive inquiry, who regretted the Emancipation Act, or who, if I may take their own professions, would have restored slavery had it been in their power. They say that if they only had the protection on the staples of the island which they enjoyed with slavery, they would prosper. It was the removal of that protection, added to the advanced price

of labor, occasioned by the emancipation of slaves, which
compelled them to surrender their accustomed market to
the cheaper slave-grown productions of Cuba and Brazil.
The number of those who are opposed to colonial protection is too small to constitute a party, and hence, that subject rarely enters into the formation of party issues of any
kind.

The party lines are most distinctly drawn between what
are known, the one as the "King's House," and the other
the "Country Party"—the former being the administration
and the latter, the opposition parties. The prominent
measure pending between them at the last Assembly, of a
strictly party character, was the retrenchment of salaries.
The country party is composed mostly of the planters and
large proprietors of land, who insist that in the present de-
pressed and impoverished condition of the island, it is impossible to pay the enormous salaries which were granted
in the days of their prosperity. They say, and with reason, that forty thousand dollars a year is too much for a
governor of four hundred thousand people, when the President of the United states, with twenty millions of subjects
receives only twenty-five thousand a year—that fifteen
thousand dollars for a Chief Justice of Jamaica, and
ten thousand for each of his associates, is extravagant,
when the Chief Justice of the highest tribunal in the
United States only gets six thousand dollars; and so

on through a succession of salaries all proportionately enormous and equally unnecessary.

The administration party, on the other hand, say that none of those holding office find their compensation exces- sive; that a residence in a hot climate, and distant from home, deserves to be well paid for; that they accepted office under the present rate, and they have a vested inter- est in their salaries, which ought not to be violated. The planters reply, that it was never their wish to have any one leave a distant home to rule them in Jamaica; in other words, they would be perfectly willing to furnish resident incumbents for all the offices on the island, for such ap- pointees would not require a premium for leaving home and living in a hot climate. Indeed, the importation of officials from the mother country has occasionally been re- sented as a great grievance by the islanders, and not with- out justice. The appointment of the present Chief Justice, Sir Joshua Rowe, is an instance. He was the first Chief Justice ever sent to Jamaica from abroad. He was ap- pointed, I believe, about fifteen years ago. Theretofore the first judicial office of the island had always been filled from the Jamaica bar. The islanders felt so outraged at this appointment, that for two years they refused to appro- priate money for his salary. Meantime he went on dis- charging his duties with noticeable ability and wisdom, and added from day to day to the number of his personal

friends, especially from among the members of the bar,
where his appointment gave most offence, until finally all
opposition disappeared, and he has since received his fifteen
thousand dollars, without a murmur against him for having
been a non-resident barrister at the time of his appointment.

After enduring their grievances as long as they thought
it became them, the country party, introduced their
bill. Of course the council, from four or five of whom
it would cut off an important moiety of their income, took
good care that the bill did not pass. The country party
sent a memorial to the Minister for the Colonies, requesting that the council might be re-constituted in a way to
enable the public sentiment of the island to have fair expression. The memorial was thrown under the minister's
table, and a speech about the colonies, from the premier in
the House of Commons, full of sympathy and figures, was
all the satisfaction which the memorialists obtained.

The country party then drew up a memorial to Parliament, setting forth the evils incident to the present organization of the council, and requesting that it should be
changed in such a way as to prevent those members whose
income, a retrenchment bill would affect, from having the
power to defeat its passage. This memorial was the prominent party measure of the last session of the Assembly.
Of course, it was resisted by the administration with all

their power. It passed, however, on the 29th of January
last, I believe, only five members voting against it.

The Colonial Standard, a journal printed at Kingston,
and the organ of the country party, commented upon this
measure as follows :—

" We observe by yesterday's proceedings, that the memorial to the Commons is to be forwarded to Mr. Roebuck
for presentation, and that to the Lords, to Lord Stanley.
The selection appears rather heterogeneous, but we are not
sorry for it. The question is not one which has any bearing on the political parties. It appeals to the independent
members of Parliament on all sides. The people of Jamaica have been subjected in their private fortunes to a
ruinous change of circumstances, and they have insisted
that the cost of government should partake of the same
cheapness as that which has been the ground-work of their
ruin. The council, composed, with two exceptions, of official and salaried individuals, possessing a personal interest
in the question, have refused to sanction any measure of
retrenchment, present or prospective ; and within the last
five years have rejected five different bills, having one or
other object. In this course they have been supported by
the Colonial office, and the only appeal lies to Parliament.
It matters not to which side of the House the conduct of
this appeal is entrusted, but a more fitting man in the
Commons than Mr. Roebuck could hardly have been selected. The analogy between the present complaint of
Jamaica and that from Canada, which was so very ably
managed by Mr. Roebuck in 1834, is complete—the only

difference being, that in Canada the council were appointed *for life*, whereas, in Jamaica, they hold their seats *at pleasure*, making the case of Jamaica, only so much stronger. Mr. Roebuck, who made good the complaints of Canada, has but to go over the same ground in exposing the grievances of Jamaica. He triumphed in the one case ; he cannot fail in the other."

This petition was presented to the House of Lords by Lord Stanley on the 6th May, on which occasion it received its *quietus* from Earl Grey, the Colonial Minister, in the following extraordinary remark, as reported by the English journals :—

" Earl Grey said, that *whatever grounds there might be for an alteration in the constitution of Jamaica*, he was not prepared to admit that there were special grounds for bringing forward the question at the present moment. The noble earl defended the conduct of the council, *who had never stood in the way of reduction or economy*."

Had the country party been successful in carrying their retrenchment bills, they would have saved, perhaps, fifty thousand dollars a year, scarcely more, rather a small matter, one would suppose, to make such a pother about. And yet it is the most direct mode left to them, of promoting their prosperity by legislation, and has been the prominent party issue among them for the past two years. A better illustration could not be desired, to show the utter impotence of the Assembly, and the over-shadowing authority of the Executive.

The country party embraces most of the English planters ; the colored people generally support the government. This surprised me at first, but I soon came to understand it. In the first place, English proprietors somehow, are always at war with the operative classes, all the world over ; at least I never heard of either of the two classes thinking that they had any community of interest. In the next place, the government have felt the necessity of conciliating the colored men in Jamaica in every possible way, and hence it is that this part of the population fill at least nine-tenths of all the offices. I think there has been a sincere desire felt by the heads of the government in England to have the blacks prosper and vindicate the philanthropic purpose which secured their liberty.

This desire has largely increased the proportion of political appointments to be made from that class. But the political and physical strength of the blacks has become formidable, and if those people were to become thoroughly alienated from their allegiance, the island would very soon become uninhabitable to English people, and its commerce would be ruined. Bearing, however, as they do, but a trifling portion of the burthen of taxation, sharing in very liberal proportions the patronage which the taxation of

others supports, and flattered by the notice and encouragement with which their loyalty is rewarded, they very
naturally ally themselves to the King's house party, upon
all questions of revenue and taxation, which, in fact, furnish
the only subjects for party controversy.

CHAPTER VI.

The poverty of Jamaica—Depreciation and diminution of exports—The market value of estates—Corresponding prostration in the other British West India colonies.

It is difficult to exaggerate, and yet more difficult to define, the poverty and industrial prostration of Jamaica. The natural wealth and spontaneous productiveness of the island are so great that no one can starve, and yet it seems as if the faculty of accumulation were suspended. All the productive power of the soil is running to waste ; the finest land in the world may be had at any price, and almost for the asking; labor receives no compensation, and the product of labor does not seem to know the way to market. Families accustomed to wealth and every luxury, have witnessed the decline of their incomes, until now, with undiminished estates, they find themselves wrestling with poverty for the commonest necessaries of life. There are no public amusements here of any kind, for amusements are purchased with the surplus wealth of people, and here there is no surplus. There was not a theatre, or a museum, or a circus, or any other place of entertainment, involving expense, open during my stay on the island. The corporation of Kingston owns a building which has been used as a theatre, and in the suburbs of the city is a plain once famous as a race course, but of the first, rats and spiders are the only tenants, and weeds and underwood have overgrown the other.

But the island abounds with more palpable, if not more significant evidences of prostration than these.

Since the year 1833, when the British Slave Emancipation Act was passed, the real estate of the island has been rapidly depreciating in value, and its productiveness has been steadily diminishing to its present comparatively ruinous standard. Whatever diversity of views may exist respecting the influence which the abolition of slavery may have had in producing this state of things, there is no doubt, I believe, entertained by any, that the passage of the Emancipation Act of 1833, was followed by the disasters I have referred to, as promptly as it could have been if it had been their cause. I will start, therefore, at that point to illustrate still further, and in another aspect, the present industrial condition of Jamaica.

Since 1832, out of the six hundred and fifty-three sugar estates then in cultivation, more than one hundred and fifty have been abandoned and the works broken up. This has thrown out of cultivation over 200,000 acres of rich land, which, in 1832, gave employment to about 30,000 laborers, and yielded over 15,000 hogsheads of sugar, and over 6,000 puncheons of rum.

During the same period, over 500 coffee plantations have been abandoned, and their works broken up. This threw out of cultivation over 200,000 acres more of land, which, in 1832, required the labor of over 30,000 men.

From an official return of the exports from the island now lying before me, I am enabled to compare the surplus production of its great staples in the three years previous to the Emancipation Act, with the exports for the three years preceding the month of October, 1848. They contrast as follows :—

Year when exported.	Sugar hhds.	Rum puns	Mo. cks.	Ginger. pounds.	Pimento pounds.	Coffee pounds.
1830....................100,205		35,625	154	1.748,800	5,560,620	22,256,950
1831..................... 94,881		36,411	230	1.614,640	3.172,320	14,055,350
1832..................... 98,686		33,645	799	2,355,560	4,024,800	19.815,010
	293,772	105,121	1,183	5,719,000	12,757,740	56,126,310
1846..... 36,223		14,895	76	1,462,600	2,997,060	6,047,150
1847..................... 48.554		18,077	22	1,524,480	2,860,140	6,421,122
1848..................... 42.212		20,194	2	820,340	5,231,908	5,684,941
	126,989	52,666	100	3,106,820	11,029,108	18,153,213

Aggregate diminution.... 166,783 | 52,455 | 1,083 | 2,862,180 | 1,628,532 | 38,973,097

By this contrast it appears that during the last three years the island has exported less than half the sugar, rum, or ginger; less than one-third the coffee; less than one-tenth the molasses; and nearly two millions of pounds less of pimento, than during the three years which preceded the Emancipation Act.

If any one reflects a moment upon the probable effects which would result from cutting off, only half the exports of such a country as the United States or England, one has less difficulty in realizing the condition of the people of Jamaica, who are not exporting much more than a third of what they have exported in the days of their prosperity.*

The political economist need not be told that such a falling off from the income of the island, must have been attended with a corresponding depreciation in the value of real estate, but no one unacquainted with the fertility and beauty, and former productiveness of Jamaica, can realize the extent of that depreciation. I will give you a few illustrations which can be relied upon.

The Spring Valley estate in the parish of St. Mary's, embracing 1,244 acres, had been sold once for £18,000 sterling. In 1842, it was abandoned, and in 1845, the freehold, including works, machinery, plantation utensils, and a water power, was sold for £1,000.

The Tremoles estate, of 1,450 acres, once worth £68,-265 sterling, has been since sold for £8,400, and would not now bring half that sum.

The Golden Valley sugar estate, containing about 1,200 acres, was sold in 1846 for £620, including machinery and works.

---

* In 1797 they exported 3,621,260 lbs. of ginger, which is one-third more than the largest quantity exported during the years I have enumerated above. In 1805 they exported 160,352 hhds. sugar, and in 1814 they exported 34,045,585 lbs. of coffee.

The Caen-wood sugar estate, which once cost £18,000, was offered by its present owners, but found no purchasers, at £1,500, and its cultivation has been abandoned.

The overseer of Friendship Valley estate used to receive a salary of £120 per annum for his services; he has been offered the whole estate within three years, for £120.

Fair Prospect estate, which used to yield five hundred hogsheads of sugar, and was valued at £40,000, was sold in 1841 for £4,000, and now would not bring anything like that sum.

Ginger Hall, which used to yield £1,200 sterling per annum, has since been sold for £1,400.

Bunker's Hill estate, which had been mortgaged for £30,000, was last sold for £2,500.

A sugar estate lying in the parish of St. Thomas, in the East, embracing 1,000 acres of land, with a good dwelling house, works, machinery, copper stills, and other appropriate fixtures, was put up at auction in 1847, in Kingston, and sold for £620.

Provision lands about the Rio Grande river, which had never been opened, and which were exceedingly productive, have been sold for one dollar per acre, and I was informed by the Governor, Sir Charles Grey, that he knew of ten thousand acres of land, lying all together, which could now be bought for £1,000, or for about fifty cents an acre; indeed, what is yet more extraordinary, a cultivated sugar estate of 2000 acres was sold only this last April for £600.

I might multiply facts of this kind without number, but it is sufficient to say, that prepared land, as fine as any under cultivation on the island, may be readily bought in unlimited quantities for five dollars an acre, while land far more productive than any in New England, may be readily had for from fifty cents to a dollar.

That the misfortunes of Jamaica may not be attributed exclusively to local causes, it is proper that I should state that the other British West India islands have all been visited by equally serious, if not the same prostrating influences, and all consider themselves ruined and helpless.

By returns recently made to the British House of Commons, it appears that, comparing the imports from British Guiana, Jamaica, and Trinidad, during the years 1831 to 1838, with the years 1844 to 1848, the production of sugar has fallen off 3,130,000 cwts., molasses 506,133 cwts., rum 3,324,627 galls., coffee 52,661,350 lbs., and the production of cotton has entirely ceased.

In 1838 there were two hundred and fifty-eight estates in Demerara and Essequibo in profitable cultivation; of these, seventy-one have been abandoned and one hundred and eleven sold under execution.

The condition of Berbice may be inferred from the following extract from the Address presented to the Governor

on the occasion of his visiting that island in the fall of
1849. It is taken from the Berbice Gazette, of October
15, 1849.

" It can but prove a source of the deepest sorrow to your
Excellency to behold in your tour of inspection throughout
this county, the rapid progress of desolation and decay,
consequent upon the measures of the Imperial Government, measures which, though intended to promote the
general interests of the empire, have been only attended
with a wholesale destruction of property here, without
producing an amount of benefit to the mass of the population at home, in any degree commensurate with such a
fearful, but one-sided sacrifice.

" We would particularly draw your Excellency's attention to the condition of the Courantyne Coast, the west
bank of the Canje Creek, and both banks of the river Berbice, and we would pray your Excellency to compare it
with the condition in which you found them on your first
visit to this country a few years ago.

" At that time your Excellency found magnificent estates,
independent and wealthy proprietors, a thriving class of
European subordinate officers, and a peasantry beyond all
comparison, the most happy and prosperous in the world.
Now, in every direction, your Excellency will only encounter
impoverished proprietors ; you will find the introduction of
intelligent European servants discontinued, the peasantry
relapsing with astonishing and most alarming rapidity into
a state of greater barbarism than at any former period, and
innumerable fine buildings and costly machinery falling

rapidly into dilapidation and decay, and approachable only by water communication, the roads and thoroughfares being quite impassable.

" That this is no over-drawn picture, your Excellency will have but too fatally conclusive proof, but it may well be inferred from the fact, that since that time, three cotton, thirty coffee, and nine sugar estates in this county alone have been totally abandoned, and are now relapsing into a wilderness."

Just before my arrival at Jamaica, the island had been visited by the Hon. E. Stanley, M.P., who was on a tour through the British possessions in the West Indies with the view of informing himself accurately of their condition. He has published the result of his observations in the form of a communication to the Hon. W. E. Gladstone. As the conclusions to which his visit lead him are quite different from those to which I have been brought by my far more limited opportunities of observation, I shall take occasion in a subsequent chapter to notice his paper again. I only refer to it now for the purpose of quoting from it some illustrations of the declining condition of Guiana. Writing to this point he says :—

" My next reference will be to an even more certain authority, the official returns of the number of estates in the colony, which at three different periods continued to export produce.

" Total number of sugar estates which made returns of produce for taxation in British Guiana were—

" In 1841, 215.   See Local Guide, page lii.

" In 1846, 208.   Taken from official returns.

" In 1848, 187.   Taken from the same.

" The diminution in the first period of five years is 7.

" The diminution in the second period of two years 21.

" In February, 1850, there were 27 estates under sequestration, of which 25 were sugar estates.

" This is so far important, that it proves the retrograde condition of a country not surpassed in point of natural advantages by any in the world ; but you will easily see that it furnishes a very inadequate idea of the real depreciation of property which has taken place, since every estate which continues to produce any crop at all—no matter how little, or at what price saleable—remains on the list as before.   A more accurate measure may perhaps be found in the following list of sales, effected before and after 1846.   It will be obvious that the number of estates thus sold and re-sold, within a period of sixteen years, must necessarily be very limited ; and consequently, that there is no room for a mere selection of isolated cases, which might give an exaggerated and unreal impression of distress.

" Indeed, even here the depreciation is not fully represented ; for, in order to be sold, an estate must find a purchaser ; and a very large proportion of those not yet wholly abandoned, are only not in the market because their owners, or the creditors of those owners, are well aware that it is useless to send them there.

" In addition to the above, I may subjoin the following communication, forwarded to me by a gentleman lately returned from Guiana :—

" ' The La Grange and Windsor Forest estates were bought by Mr. Cruikshank for £25,000 and £40,000, in 1838 and 1840, respectively. The two were sold together, a few weeks ago, for £11,000 nominally ; but this price included a claim for £5,000 due to the purchaser, making the actual purchase money £6,000, or something less than one-tenth of the original value.'

" Showing a fall in aggregate value of something like 90 per cent ! Will any one say after this, that the statements which reach them of colonial distress are exaggerated or over-colored ? Take now the description given by a member of the Court of Policy, Mr. White, himself a planter, addressing the·Combined Court in presence of the Governor ; and let it be noticed that the accuracy of his assertions appears nowhere to have been disputed in the subsequent debate :—

" ' To show how property in this country had depreciated in value within the last few years, it appeared to be necessary only to compare the present value of that property with what it brought a few years ago. The value of fixed property—sugar estates—before emancipation, was estimated at twenty millions of pounds sterling, or twice the value of the slaves, as they were appraised by the commissioners. But what was the value of that same property now ? There were still 220 estates in the colony. If the sales which had taken place within the last year were to be taken as a criterion of the present value of property—and he thought they could very properly be taken as a criterion—it would be found that the average value of estates did not exceed £3,000. It was only the other day

that two large estates which, within his recollection, a few
years ago, would have brought £40,000, were sold for
£3,000 each. Therefore, taking £3,000 as the average
value of estates, the real value of estates here, including
cotton and coffee estates, was £660,000; that was to say,
property which some years ago would have brought twenty
millions sterling, had been, in consequence of the measures
of the British Government, reduced in value to £660,000.
That showed the utter annihilation which had taken place
in the value of property in the colony. There was another
point which would also show the great depreciation which
had taken place in the value of property. In the petition
to which he had already referred, it was stated that the
gross annual value of produce of the colony in 1846, was
$3,500,000, or £700,000 sterling. Now, he believed he
had shown the value of all landed property in the country,
taking the value of the estate to be £3,000, was £660,000.
That was, the value of the sugar estates in the colony was
only £660,000, while the produce of a year was £700,000.
In fact, the landed property in this country was not worth
one year's purchase!' "

It is easy to see that such a general depreciation in the
price of productive property anywhere, must leave poverty
and ruin on its path, but adequately to realize the financial
reverses of this gem of the ocean, it is necessary to appreciate its exceeding fertility and unequalled natural resources.
I will briefly allude to some of the most prominent indica-
tions of both.

CHAPTER VII.

Physical resources of Jamaica—Soil—Fruits—Vegetables—Drugs
——Trees—Irrigation—Rivers—Difficulties of transportation——
Harbors—Mines.

JAMAICA embraces about 4,000,000 acres of land, of
which there are not, probably, any ten lying adjacent to
each other, which are not susceptible of the highest cultivation, while not more than 500,000 acres have ever been
reclaimed, or even appropriated.

The quality and productiveness of the soil may be inferred in part, from what I have said of its exports. Sugar
retoons here, on most plantations, three or four times. I
myself picked some cotton of a superior quality, which had
been planted more than ten years. Very little of the soil
has been manured, or requires to be, and such a thing as
an exhausted estate is hardly known. The negroes sometimes exhaust the three or four acres of which they may
have become proprietors, by covering the ground with every
variety of fruit and vegetable, and by planting anew, after
every crop, without giving the soil either rest or restoratives.
But these exceptions are of trifling importance. Vegetation

here is not suspended by the approach of winter, which averages a temperature only ten or fifteen degrees lower than that of summer. Planting and harvesting go on throughout the year.

The richness of the soil may be inferred from a usage which has existed since long previous to the abolition of slavery, of setting apart to the negroes one day in seven for the cultivation of their own little grounds from which they gather nearly their entire support. On Saturdays, they are never expected to work for any one but themselves. They devote that day to tilling their grounds and marketting their produce. This one day's labor in each week is all they require to keep up to the highest power of production, from three to five, and sometimes ten acres of provision grounds.

The fruits of the island are of infinite variety, and most of them grow spontaneously, or with very little culture; each month having its own peculiar harvest. Among those fruits which grow in greatest abundance and perfection, are the pine apple, shadduck, orange, pomegranate, fig, grenedillo, cashew apple, banana, star apple, chirimoya, tamarind, cocoa nut, olive, date, plantain, mulberry, akee, jack fruit, bread fruit, and every variety of melons, grapes, pears, plums, mangos, &c.

Among vegetables most easy of cultivation, are potatoes, yams, cassava, peas and beans of every variety, all the common table vegetables of the United States, ochro, choco, calalue, and a curious variety of salads.   Maize and Indian corn grow here luxuriantly.   The Guinea grass, which is superior for grazing purposes to any other, grows wild to the height of five and six feet.

The island also abounds in dye stuffs, drugs and spices of the greatest value ; to these may be added the aloe, ginger, cochineal, spikenard, liquorice root, castor oil nut, vanilla, peppers of every variety, arrow root, ippecacuanha, jalap, cassia, senna, and many others, of which I have no know-ledge.   I have already· referred to the immense crops of pimento which used to be gathered here, and which in 1848, in spite of the general agricultural depression upon the island, amounted to over five millions of pounds.   I learned a fact in the natural history of this spice which was new to me, and may be new to many of my readers. It was communicated by Mr. Richard Hill, the colored gentleman to whose accomplishments in natural history I have already alluded.

The island of Jamaica furnishes nine-tenths of all the pimento that is the subject of commerce throughout the world.   And yet, says Mr. Hill, there is not a pimento walk on the island which has been cultivated from seed planted by human hands.   On the contrary, all the seed is scattered about with the *rejectamenta* of the birds, and when it comes up, the bushes and shrubbery by which it happens

to be surrounded are cut away from about it, and thus the
pimento walk is laid out. The same thing, he said, was
true of the guava. He intimated an impression that a proper analysis of the soil in which the seed germinated would
probably reveal the secret, hitherto inviolate, by the aid of
which the pimento could be cultivated from its seed.

This statement becomes the more astonishing when the
fact is considered that Jamaica has exported over three
millions of pounds of this spice in a single year.

The forests of Jamaica abound with the rarest cabinet
woods, in wonderful variety. I was shown a beautiful box,
the top of which was inlaid with thirty different choice and
rich indigenous specimens.

Among the trees of most value in various ways may be
mentioned the bread fruit tree, which takes a fine polish ;
the satin wood ; the cedar, which grows to an immense
size ; the cotton tree, the body of which is cut out by the
negroes for canoes ; the bamboo, one of the most useful
trees on the island ; the trumpet tree, the bark of which
is used for cordage and the body for other purposes ; the
black and green ebony ; lignumvitæ ; the palmetto, which
sometimes grow one hundred and forty feet in height, and
others. The mahogany is native to Jamaica, but is now
getting quite scarce, so extensively has it been cut and exported during the past forty years.

It is proper to say that some of the parishes require irri-

gation during a portion of the year. This necessity is confined almost exclusively to the south side of the island, districts which sometimes are not visited with rain for three
or four months. Spanishtown and Kingston, and their
respective suburbs, oftentimes experience these prolonged
droughts, and without irrigation all cultivation in their vicinity is not unfrequently entirely suspended for a short period,
while in the adjacent parishes, at the same time perhaps,
there will be frequent and sometimes excessive rains. In
one hour a person may drive from Spanishtown, where
everything is parched and perishing, into St. Thomas, in
the Vale, where the most luxuriant foliage and abounding
rivulets and meadow streams indicate frequent and copious
showers. In the dry parishes however, the want of moisture
that is not repaired by the heavy dews which are providen-
tially sent during the winter season, may be supplied by
irrigation at very inconsiderable expense ; for the whole
island abounds in water at all times. It is traversed by over
two hundred streams, forty of which are from twenty-five to
a hundred feet in breadth, and, it deserves to be mentioned,
furnish water power sufficient to manufacture everything produced by the soil, or consumed by the inhabitants. Far less
expense than is usually incurred on the same surface in
the United States for manure, would irrigate all the dry
lands of the island, and enable them to defy the most protracted droughts with which it is ever visited.

The facilities for transportation in Jamaica are exceedingly limited. With the exception of the fifteen miles of railroad, there is not, to my knowledge, a stage coach or regular periodical conveyance to be found in Jamaica ; nor does any steam or other boat ply at stated periods between any of her ports. Of course, therefore, the expense of getting about is very great, and the intercourse between the opposite extremities of the island, quite limited—more so than between the Atlantic shore of the United States and the Mississippi valley, and rather more expensive.

While man has done so little for the internal improvement of the island, Providence has benignantly indented its shore with sixteen secure harbors and some thirty bays, all affording good anchorage, as if it were designed to provide against the indolence and supineness of her inhabitants by inviting to her shores the enterprise and capital of other nations.

Besides the productiveness of its surface, this island unquestionably abounds in mineral wealth. As slavery never can beget or procure mechanical skill, the mineral regions have never been thoroughly explored or worked, nor their value understood ; but I have good reason to believe that its copper mines are inferior in richness to none in the world, and that coal will be mined here extensively before many years.

Such are some of the natural resources of this dilapidated

and poverty-stricken country.   Capable as it is of producing
almost everything, and actually producing nothing which
might not become a staple with a proper application of
capital and skill, its inhabitants are miserably poor, and
daily sinking deeper and deeper into the utter helplessness
of abject want.

Magnas inter opes inops.

Shipping has deserted her ports ; her magnificent plantations of·sugar and coffee are running to weeds ; her private
dwellings are falling to decay ; the comforts and luxuries
which belong to industrial prosperity have been cut off,
one by one, from her inhabitants ; and the day, I think, is
at hand when there will be none left to represent the wealth,
intelligence and hospitality for which the Jamaica planter
was once so distinguished.

Why is this ?   Is any one to blame for it, and can human
agency extend any relief, and if any, what is it ?   These
are questions which have been much considered, and have
received so great a diversity of answers, that I indulge the
hope of being pardoned for adding one to the number.

CHAPTER VIII.

The decline of Jamaica explained—The complaints of the planters
—The remedies proposed by the planters—The real difficulties in Jamaica stated—First, the degradation of labor.

THE present ruinous condition of Jamaica is ascribed by
its inhabitants mainly to three causes, the abolition of
slavery in 1834, the inadequate compensation paid to the
owners of the slaves, and to the repeal of the protective
duty on British colonial sugar.

1st. The abolition of slavery they aver, caused the price
of labor to advance beyond the point of successful competition with countries where slavery was tolerated. It became impossible, as they claimed, for a Jamaica planter,
with free labor, to raise sugar for anything like the prices
at which it was sold by the planters of Cuba, Brazil, and
Porto Rico.

2d. England, they say, paid them but a small proportion of the value of the slaves when she emancipated them.
The Commissioners appraised the slave property of all the

British West Indies at £43,104,889 8s. 6d., and the government finally allowed the owners only £16,638,937 8s. 1¾d., or less than fifty per cent., whereby the slave-holders sustained a loss of over £26,000,000 in addition to the loss, supposed to be twice as much more, sustained from the depreciation in the value of the fixed property, much of which, this change in the character of the labor rendered no longer productive or available.

3rd. In 1846, Parliament passed a law reducing the duties on sugar, by which slave grown sugars were admitted into the British market at a corresponding reduction of price. The planters complained that the necessity of using free labor compelled them to expend more in raising their crops, while the removal of the protective duties compelled them to accept less for them when gathered. This act is now their great grievance. They do not ask the mother country to change its general free trade policy, but they insist that the right of the planters to receive full compensation for their slaves was recognized by the government, that such compensation was not paid in money, but that a prohibitory duty on slave grown sugar was offered them as an important part of their indemnification. They farther state, that by opening the British markets to slave grown sugar, they are propagating and fostering an institution, the suppression of which was the avowed motive of the government for stripping the planters of their slave property by the Emancipation Act of 1834.*

I believe I have here given a full and perfectly fair statement of the causes to which the Jamaicans as a body, attribute their ruin. It is a fair reflexion of the sentiment of their journals, and corresponds with the view of Mr. Stanley, who has volunteered to be their champion and apologist. It is a view which leaves them nothing to do, and therefore is very naturally acceptable to a West Indian. They fold their arms under the conviction that no efforts of theirs can arrest the decay and dissolution going on about them, and that nothing but home legislation, nay, nothing but protection to their staples, can protect them from hopeless and utter ruin.

This has seemed to me a most gross and extraordinary

---

* The following is the material clause of this Act, certainly one of the very most momentous measures ever adopted by any legislative body. It directly set at liberty some 800,000 human beings, and destroyed a title to over three millions of property. The bill was submitted in 1833 by Lord Stanley, then Secretary for the Colonies.

"Be it enacted, that all and every, the persons who, on the first day of August, one thousand eight hundred and thirty-four, shall be holden in slavery within any such British Colony as aforesaid, shall, upon and from and after the said first day of August, one thousand eight hundred and thirty-four, become and be to all intents and purposes free, and discharged of and from all manner of slavery, and shall be absolutely and forever manumitted ; and that the children thereafter born to any such persons, and the offspring of such children, shall in like manner be free from birth ; and that from and after the first day of August, one thousand eight hundred and thirty-four, slavery shall be, and is hereby utterly and forever abolished and declared unlawful throughout the British colonies, plantations and possessions abroad."

This bill also provided for a system of apprenticeship which was to last twelve years, and then give place to unrestricted freedom. This system worked so badly that after a trial of four years it was abandoned, and on the 1st of August, 1838, the freedmen of all the British Colonies were made fully and unconditionally free.

delusion, though it seems to be one which is hurrying on the result they deprecate. The downward tendencies of the island cannot be more rapid than they are at present, and it is possible that the present population will not be able to arrest them without help from the government. If so, then the ruin of Jamaica is inevitable, for nothing is less probable than that England will return to the protective system of 1814, or compel the consumers of sugar in England to pay a tax of over $25,000,000, merely to sustain the proprietors of sugar and coffee estates in the West India islands.

I will not attempt to conjecture what a change in the revenue policy of Great Britain might effect for her colonies, nor how far a restoration of slavery would contribute to repair the losses which its abolition is supposed by some to have caused ; but of two things I am clear. I am clear that neither course would have saved them from bankruptcy, for they were all mortgaged for more than they were worth at the time slavery was abolished and when their staples were protected in the English markets by prohibitory duties. I am also clear that if Jamaica was an American State, she would speedily be more productive and valuable than any agricultural portion of the United States of the same dimensions, and that neither the Emancipation Bill of '33, nor the Sugar Duties Bill of '46, are fatal obstacles to a prosperity far exceeding anything which Jamaica has ever known.

An American has but to glance his eye over the industry of this island, to discern ample causes for its declining condition, which are quite independent of those to which it has been charged. While those continue, no home legislation, in my judgment, can make the island permanently prosperous. If they are removed, I might say with almost equal confidence, that no home legislation could prevent their becoming prosperous. I will mention some of these causes which most impressed me, and were most frequently forced upon my attention.

First in importance I reckon the degrading estimate placed upon every species of agricultural labor by the white population. It is well known that the laborer belongs to a proscribed class throughout the British dominions, and that no merit or accomplishment will wipe out the disgrace of such a connexion. That feeling, of course, is very much more inexorable here among the planters, who have been accustomed mainly to slave labor. They would, as a class, sooner beg than hold the plough or ply the hoe. Of course one never sees a white laborer on their estates, and the colored people have no competition for wages except with persons of their own complexion. It is unnecessary to add, that such an estimate of labor among the whites has a most pernicious effect upon the blacks. They, with the average sequence of negro logic, infer that if gentlemen never work, they have only to abstain from work to

be gentlemen. Again, they revolt from a service which
they think degrades them, and are disinclined to labor for
others more than is absolutely necessary for their own
maintenance.   They render their services without any
alacrity, and without any desire or effort to have it reward
the employer.

It is owing to this unworthy pride on the part of the
white people, and the enervating effect of their example
upon the blacks, that the former, as a mass, are almost
entirely unproductive, and the latter far less productive
than they should be or would be, if within the influence of
a healthier public opinion.   Between the two, there is no
intellect invested in the industry of the island.   The
planter does not attend personally to the culture of his
estates, and, of course, does not avail himself of his superior
capacity to select and devise modes of economizing labor,
and in multiplying the productive power of his land.   The
operatives have no interest to diminish the amount of labor
required, for that, they fancy, would bring down wages,
which are now so low as hardly to be worth collecting
after they are earned ; but if they had, they are mostly too
ignorant to make the attempt successfully.   The whites are
generally too proud or too lazy to supervise and teach the
black, and if they were not, they also are too ignorant to do it,
for they rarely give more thought to the mechanics of their
estates, or possess more skill in managing them, than the

more intelligent of the negroes employed by them. The consequence is, that while the cost of labor has been advancing, there has been no advance whatever in the mechanical and implemental economics of the island.*

I could not perceive that sixteen years of freedom had advanced the dignity of labor, or of the laboring classes one particle. That fell legacy which slavery always leaves behind it, I found here, neither wasted nor reduced. The operative occupies a decidedly lower social position in Jamaica now, than he does in South Carolina. The degrading effects of slavery upon free labor are written all over the Slave States of the American Union, and are familiar to all my readers. Those effects, aggravated by the heats of a warmer sun, and mitigated by few of the social and political influences which are constantly operating upon the laboring classes in the United States, I found

---

* An incident came under my observation one day in Spanishtown which in part illustrates what I have been saying, and as a commentary upon the habitual indolence of the people, may be worth making "a note of." I wished to leave that place one morning by the railroad in the seven o'clock train for Kingston, and the evening previous requested my landlady to have a carriage ordered to take me to the cars in season. When I asked in the morning for my carriage, I was told that none could be procured at so early an hour. Upon farther inquiry it appeared that the negroes would not mount their boxes before nine or ten o'clock, and of course the white proprietors would, on no terms, be seen driving a hack. So I was obliged to find my way to the cars as best I could, "with the tandem that nature gave me." If there had been no train of cars leaving Spanishtown at this hour, and no habitual call for coaches thus early, I should have attached less importance to the incident, but the failure of my application made it apparent that their indolence was as obstinate as their pride, and that the daily prospect of a fare was not a sufficient inducement to make either whites or blacks, leave their beds to man a hackney coach at six o'clock in the morning.

perpetuated here in all their vigor, neither weakened nor
amelioriated in the least, apparently, among the whites, in
the long period during which the labor of the island has
been performed exclusively by freedmen.

CHAPTER IX.

Absenteeism and Middlemen.

I HAD no occasion to exaggerate the consequences of that fell inheritance which slavery always entails upon the nation that tolerates it—the degradation of field labor; for, in the first place, it is well-known, at least by my own countrymen, that the evil can hardly be over-stated, and in the next place, many other causes of the prostration I see about me, might be enumerated, which must have dragged this island down to poverty and ruin, though no change had ever been made in the character of the labor employed or in the tariff by which it was protected. Of these, the next in importance to the one I have already mentioned, is the non-residence of the landholders. I have ascertained that nine-tenths of the land under cultivation before the Emancipation Act, was owned by absentees, and that that proportion has not been diminished materially, except by the abandonment of properties, as it is called—that is, the ceasing to cultivate them, selling off their moveable improvements and furniture, and surrendering them to weeds and under-brush. This disposition has been made, as I have before stated, of some 400,000 acres.

But the proportion of absentees has been made up since, by the purchase of depreciated estates upon the foreclosure of mortgages given to secure absent money-lenders, of whose operations I shall speak presently. There are, therefore, very few extensive proprietors of land among the resident population of the island.

The blighting influence of absenteeism, and its tendency to drive from a country its wealth, its intelligence, its ingenuity, and its patriotism, have been made familiar to the world by the unhappy experience of Ireland. I need not speak of them therefore in detail. There are some features of the system in its operation here, which are not quite so obvious. Most of the land is held by English proprietors, whose residence has usually been distant from it, at least one month's sail. This involves the necessity of employing a resident attorney, to take a proprietary supervision of the estate, whose duty it is to employ an overseer to conduct its tillage, and who is expected to advise the proprietor of everything connected with its management, and to transmit the proceeds of the crops whenever there are any to transmit.

The overseer occupies the mansion, usually a handsome house, where he is personally attended by from three to five, and not unfrequently twice that number of servants, and as many horses, with the aid of which he keeps an eye to the culture and harvesting of crops, the employment of operatives, and the devising of excuses for the short returns which are sure to follow the indifference, laziness, and dishonesty which in nine cases out of ten characterize his management.

But this hierarchy of agencies is not yet complete. Each overseer has from one to three bookkeepers, as they are called, the number depending upon the size and productiveness of the estate. I do not know of an estate with less than two, and I presume they usually exceed than fall short of that number. It is their duty, primarily, to keep the accounts, and incidentally, to act as checks upon the overseer ; and it is the duty of the attorney to act as a check upon both. These different agents have to be paid a compensation averaging for each estate throughout the island, over $3000 a year. This sum has to be earned, not to pay the interest on the land or the improvements ; not to pay for the laborers to cultivate it ; not to bring its produce to market, but mostly, if not exclusively, for services made necessary by the absence of the proprietor from the island.

His estate has to make a profit of nearly three thousand dollars upon the investment before he can receive a farthing. If it fails to net that amount, it is insolvent, and if the proprietor have no other resources, he must mortgage or sell at once. To escape the necessity of choosing between such disheartening alternatives, he is compelled to draw everything from the estate and return nothing. He turns all its produce into money, and ships it home as fast as possible, not leaving it one unnecessary day to circulate in the commerce of the island. None of it is invested in improvements, in labor-saving machinery, in manuring, or in any other way, for the benefit of the estate, but all goes off to keep down a foreign interest account, to pay off mortgages or to be expended upon his support elsewhere.

Of course the estate gradually depreciates in productiveness and value under such a process of depletion, and the alternatives which the planter seeks to avoid, he has only postponed; he is finally compelled either to borrow or sell. He usually prefers the former course, and this leads me to notice another of the series of influences which have proved so fatal to the prosperity of Jamaica; but before doing so, I feel impelled to notice a defence of this absenteeism which has been interposed by Mr. Stanley in his recent communication to Mr. Gladstone, to which I have already referred. As he is the accepted champion of the colonists, both in his literary and in his representative capacity, it is proper that I should notice what are his grounds for defending a practice which his ruined clients, and all who are the victims of it, are accustomed to look upon as the greatest of political calamities.   Mr. Stanley, upon this topic, writes as follows :—

" ' The planters are absentees.'   Undoubtedly ; and as long as their incomes enable them to reside in England, it is not likely that they will be otherwise.   Europeans do not live under a tropical sun, debarred alike from the exercises of country life, and the resources of a great city, injuring their constitutions, weakening their bodily powers, and with the loss of those powers, losing also the energy of mind, which distinguishes them at home, without some valid reason of necessity or of profit.   Nor am I disposed to deny that in many, perhaps in most cases, their estates would be benefitted by their presence.   But can we expect them to become *bona fide* settlers ?   Is it desirable that they should do so ?   I doubt it ; and for this reason : Though the traveller in a tropical colony is repeatedly thrown in contact with men who will assure him that the climate is perfectly healthy—that it is nonsense to talk of life being shorter there than in England—that they have never been ill in their lives, &c., &c.,—yet he has to remember that these old residents are the exceptions, and not the rule ; and that while most of those who remain in the country will agree in the same story, he has seen or heard nothing of the far more numerous class who, having resided a few years, and failed to endure the change, have either found themselves under the necessity of returning to England, or of taking a still longer and more inevitable journey. Very few Europeans can take up their abode permanently in the West Indies, without at least some intervals of re s dence in a colder climate. With the Cuban planter the case is different ; yet the Cuban planter, settled all the year round at the Havanna, sees hardly more of his estate than the Englishman. But even supposing that after many years and frequent deaths, a race of British proprietors had become permanent residents of Jamaica and Guiana, and thereby accustomed to the climate, I believe the change would not be found beneficial. In fact the process of acclimation to an Englishman, necessarily involves the loss of his European energies, and an approximation to the bodily condition of the people among whom he lives. There is even now a large Creole population of white descent ; and assuredly their best friends will not say of them, that in energy or industry they approach the natives of the north. I have myself seen Americans from the United States, not the most naturally indolent of men, settled in the cities of the Spanish Main, and after long residence, hardly distinguished in point of activity from the people among whom they live.

" On this ground then, I doubt the advantage as well as the possibility of establishing in the West Indies a class of resident English landowners ; and I utterly and altogether deny the assertion, that the unproductive nature of West Indian property is owing to the absenteeism of its owners."

In other words, Mr. Stanley argues that the Englishman cannot preserve his physical and mental vigor in the tropical climates ; therefore absenteeism is not one of the causes of the unproductiveness of West Indian property. I submit that this premise is not quite broad enough for the conclusion. It is a perfectly good reason for a man to give for not going to a tropical climate, that it does not agree with his constitution, but that would be no reason for his drawing five or six fair profits off his estates there, one for himself, one for his attorney, another for his overseer, and two or three others for his book-keepers, without enduring any of the exposure or exercising any of the supervision and forethought which is necessary to earn even a single profit in any other part of the globe. The insalubrity of a place is a good reason for keeping away from it, and it is a good reason for compensating those who do go to it, liberally ; it is a good reason for those who cannot or dare not live in it, to sell out to those who dare, but we do not see with what face the non-resident proprietor can step up and ask the government to give him a monopoly which will enable him to hire others to do all his working and thinking, and to pocket cent. per cent. on his investment besides.

But Mr. Stanley goes farther, he claims, in substance, that the supervision and management of an agent is as faithful as that of his principal, and that agents and servants are as thrifty and as serviceable under the eye of an agent as under the eye of the real party interested in the product of their labor ; for he substantially affirms both these propositions, when he denies the assertion that any of the unproductiveness of the British West India islands is

owing to absenteeism. Nay, he does not leave his readers
merely to infer his sentiments upon this point; for in the
paragraph which follows the extract above quoted, he adds:

" But another line of attack is sometimes taken. It is
not so much the absence of landowners from their properties, we are told, as the waste that takes place upon them
—which prevents their attaining their proper value in the
market. It is difficult to reconcile these two charges with
one another; still more difficult to understand how the
latter should ever have been received? In what is this re-
puted extravagance to show itself? It would be a difficult
matter for an agent or overseer living on an estate in the
country, isolated from his neighbors, occupied with the
practical details of superintendence, and probably at a
considerable distance from the capital of the colony, to live
expensively if he wished it. The land supplies him with
almost all that he requires; he obtains the necessaries of
life without paying for them, and the luxuries he would not
find it easy to obtain at all. This, however, is a simple
matter of observation and of fact; and I will only say,
that during a journey which occupied several weeks in
Jamaica, and in which I visited a large proportion of the
best cultivated estates in the island, I never saw any of
these signs of lavish or careless expenditure by agents or
overseers—which having possibly occurred to a certain extent in days long previous to emancipation, have now been
revived as a subject of attack against a class whose reduced
means alone suffice to vindicate their character in this
respect."

Though Mr. Stanley professes to speak upon this point from personal observation, I incline to doubt whether he brought to the investigation, either the zeal or the patience which sustained him in collecting evidences of the poverty and prostration of the colonies. If he had, I am sure his experience would have been less inconsistent with mine, as well as with all the presumptions suggested by the observations of experienced men.

I hardly conversed with any man of substance in Jamaica on this subject who had not some story, within his own observation, to tell me, of the carelessness, the improvidence and corruption of these middlemen, in whose hands was the control of most of the real estate of the island. It is a common thing, I was told, for the overseers to keep down the returns, and to increase the expenses of estates, by devices perfectly familiar here, until the owner becoming anxious to rid himself of the cares of a property which yielded nothing but anxiety and expense, should send out authority to sell it for what it would bring. These overseers would then buy it in themselves at a ruinous sacrifice. I lived myself for some time here in a house of which a man had been robbed by this very process.

But even when there is no fraud, there is great inattention and heedlessness, such as no proprietor would ever be guilty of himself. I met a gentleman one day, who had recently come from England to look after an estate, which was annually sinking money without any apparent cause. His first step on his arrival was to visit his attorney, who resided at Spanishtown, the estate itself being some sixty miles distant. On inquiring about the condition of the property, the attorney was obliged to make the mortifying confession that he had never seen it, and could give no information about it. Nor was this altogether an exceptional case, for I venture to say, that not half of the estates are visited by their attornies once a year. How these facts could have escaped Mr. Stanley's observation, as I presume they did, I find it difficult to understand, and his oversight is more to be regretted, as with his ample opportunities for reaching authentic facts upon the subject, he might have escaped the gross misapprehension into which he has fallen, and might also have supplied his countrymen who are interested in West Indian property, with some information by which they could profit.

For my own part, I can see no one aspect in which absenteeism is not a calamity to the colonies, nor do I think it easy to ascribe to it too large a proportion of their present distresses.

CHAPTER X.

Encumbered Estates.

ANOTHER of the calamities which hang like plummets at the heels of enterprise in Jamaica, is the encumbered condition of the land. I was surprised to learn, that there is scarcely an estate upon the island which is not mortgaged, or which has not been sold under a mortgage sale. I should distrust the accuracy of my information, if I had not received it from the most authentic and reliable sources. I was assured by the Attorney General of the island, an Irish barrister of high standing, and the highest authority upon a matter of this sort, that an unencumbered estate of any size or value, was hardly to be found here. I verified his statements in numerous ways, and by inquiries addressed to those most likely to be informed upon such a subject, and found no difference of opinion about it. A gentleman who had been for many years a resident upon the island, admitted to me, after some reflection, that he could not call to mind an exception—a single large estate that was unencumbered.

What makes this evil the greater is, that, in most instances, the mortgages are for much larger amounts than
the mortgaged property is worth. The reason is, that
most of the mortgages were given before the abolition
of slavery and the subsequent depreciation of property,
to which I have referred, and when West Indian estates
were a popular security in Mincing lane and Downing
street. I say the mortgages were given before, because
it has not been possible since then, to borrow money to any
extent upon Jamaica property, so serious and even ruinous
have been the losses sustained in consequence of the rapid
depreciation of real estate since that event.*

The way the property became so encumbered is worth
tracing out, for it goes farther than anything else to explain the poverty I see about me.

Jamaica does not furnish a sufficiently extended market
for all her staples. Of course, therefore, they have to go
abroad or be wasted. The British Parliament had, for
some thirty years previous to the year 1846, invited them
to England, by protective duties, discriminating Colonial
from foreign products, to the advantage of the former.
For the reasons to which I have alluded, the landholders
were compelled long before the abolition of slavery, to

---

* Not only cannot the individual landholders borrow money upon their real
estate, but the government itself has failed to effect a loan within the past year,
upon the security of the island, and an extra session of the Assembly has been
called to meet the emergency.

raise money by loans, or sell their lands. But selling was merely changing the person of the borrower, for to borrow became sooner or later an inevitable necessity, under the system of absenteeism by which the island was cursed. The lenders were naturally those who traded with the island, the consignees of produce, who would begin by making advances, and end by taking mortgages. They would lend the planters money, upon their stipulating to send all their produce to the lender's house, in London, to be sold, and to buy from them whatever in their particular line of business the estate consumed. These arrangements were generally made, so that the London trader would get whatever commission he chose to take for selling the produce, and whatever price he chose to ask for his own merchandise. The planter's candle, therefore, would thus be burning at both ends, and I must say, in the middle also; for he produced, sold and bought at a disadvantage.

Of course, it would not take long, under such financiering, for the proprietor to get a larger load upon his back than he could carry alone. He would soon experience a necessity for more money than could be raised upon his consignments. His consignees, anxious to secure their control over his business, are happy to lend him what he requires, if he will secure the loan by a mortgage upon his estate. He has no other security to give, and consents.

From that moment his thraldom becomes complete, and insolvency, sooner or later, is almost inevitable.

It was in this way, precisely, that nearly every considerable estate in Jamaica became encumbered, before the abolition of slavery, for nearly its full value at that time. Then came the Emancipation Act, and the consequent fall in the price of real estate, which has been steadily obeying a downward tendency, until it no longer possesses one-tenth of its former value.

The change wrought by this law in 1846, in the character of the labor, would necessarily have produced some confusion for a time, and perhaps serious pecuniary losses were inevitable, but both the confusion and the losses were aggravated to a ruinous extent by the large indebtedness of the island. The planters had nothing in their hands to defend themselves with when the blow came—neither money nor credit. Had they been out of debt, they could have sustained themselves upon the money they received from the government for their slaves, and what they could have borrowed upon their land. But as they were situated, all the money which was allowed them by government, as emancipation money, had to be applied at once to the reduction of the mortgage debts—for the extinction of which, however, they were altogether inadequate ; so that the planter, after parting with all his slaves, was left under a heavy debt to contend against a new system of labor and a depreciating property.* These are facts which never, so far as I know, have been taken into account by those who have charged the ruin of Jamaica to the abolition of slavery. They point to her large exports previous to 1832, and insist that the island at that time was wealthy and prosperous. They then refer to the reduced exports since the abolition of slavery, and arguing *post hoc propter hoc*, deplore the poverty which that event has brought upon the country.

*DISTRIBUTION OF SLAVE COMPENSATION.—The Commissioners for the apportionment of the sum of £20,000,000 granted by parliament as compensation to slave-owners, under the act 3 & 4 Will. 4, cap. 73, at the conclusion of their labors, issued the following table. It shows the average value of a slave in each colony; the number of slaves in each by the last registration; the total value of the slaves, supposing the annual value of each were realized; and the proportion of the £20,000,000 to which each colony is entitled.

Colouy.	Average value of a slave from 1822 to 1830.			Number of slaves by last registration in thiscountry	Relative value of the slaves.			Proportion of the £2,000,000 to which each olocny is entitled.			
	£	s.	d.		£	s.	d.	£	s.	d.	
Bermuda, ...	27	4	11¾	4,203	114,527	7	5¼	50584	7	0½	.41
Bahamas, ...	29	18	9¾	9,705	290,573	15	3¾	128340	7	5¾	.47
Jamaica	44	15	2¼	311,692	13,951,139	2	3	6161927	5	10⅛	.58
Hondura, ...	120	4	7½	1,920	230,844	0	0	101958	19	7½	.92
Virgin Islands,......	31	16	1¾	5,192	165,143	9	2	72940	8	5¼	.76
Antigua, ...	32	12	10½	29,537	964,198	0	10½	425866	7	0¼	.13
Montserrat,.........	36	17	10¾	6,355	234,466	8	0¼	103558	18	5	.38
Nevis, ...	39	3	11¾	8,722	341,893	6	3½	151007	2	11¾	.35
St. Christopher's,...	36	6	10¾	20,660	750,840	7	1	331630	10	7¼	.82
Dominica, ...	43	8	7½	14,384	624,715	2	0	275923	12	3½	30
Barbadoes,.........	47	1	3½	82,807	3,897,276	19	0½	1721345	19	7	.87
Grenada,...........	59	6	0	23.536	1,395,684	16	0	616444	17	7	.03
St. Vincent's,.......	58	6	8	22,997	1,341,491	13	4	592508	18	0¼	.93
Tobago,............	45	12	0½	11.621	629,941	16	2½	234064	4	11⅔	.55
St. Lucia,..........	56	18	7	13,348	759,890	10	4	335627	15	11¾	.13
Trinidad, ...	105	4	5¼	22,359	2,352,655	18	0⅜	1089119	1	3½	.11
British Guiana,....	114	11	5¼	84,915	9,729,047	13	5¼	4297117	10	6½	30
Cape of Good Hope	73	98	11	38,427	2,824,224	7	9	1247401	0	7¾	.76
Mauritius,..........	69	14	3	68,613	4,783,183	15	3	2112632	10	11¾	.06
								defic'nt fractions			08
				780,993	45,281,738	15	10¼	20,000,000	0	0	

If the premises upon which this argument is based were sound, it would be conclusive evidence to many minds, of the impolicy of emancipating the slaves, but when it is considered that the island was utterly insolvent the day the emancipation bill passed, that nearly every estate was mortgaged for more than it was worth, and was liable for more interest than it could possibly pay, the question assumes a very different aspect. Yet such was the fact. It will not be disputed by any who are at all informed upon the subject, that the whole real estate under culture in Jamaica in 1832, would not have sold for enough to pay off its encumbrances. This fact must have been disclosed sooner or later, even though slavery had been permitted to continue. Bankruptcy was inevitable, and the rapid depreciation of real estate, would of course have been one of the first fruits of such a catastrophe.

Had the indemnification money paid for the slaves been sufficient to pay off the debts of the island, and emancipated the planters from the tyranny of usurers and mortgagees, it is possible that they might have kept out of debt, and thus have escaped some of their heaviest expenses. They could have bought in the cheapest, and sold in the dearest market, and they could have escaped many heavy commissions to which their obligations to the foreign commission merchant compelled them to submit. But as it was, they actually purchased their credit. They got their notes extended upon condition that they bought of their creditors all their supplies—for which they were sure to be charged always the highest market prices—and sent to them all their produce to sell, for which they were charged heavy commissions. These expenses might have been avoided if the islanders had been out of debt, but the indemnification money they received was far from affording the required relief. It reduced, but did not extinguish the mortgages, and in a very few years the money was gone, and no one could tell where, or for what. Meantime, the property depreciated in value to such an extent, that it could not be sold; the planters were compelled to draw every thing they could from their properties, exhausting them at every turn to meet their interest debts, and to prevent a forced and ruinous sale. In this way it is, that the downward tendencies of the island, which were derived from a degraded system of labor, and non-resident proprietorships, have been accelerated by the indebtedness of the planters.

That the connexion between the planter and the home merchant, as he is called, may be better understood by American readers, I may as well here add a brief statement of the usual mode in which their business with each other is transacted, which will illustrate what I have stated. I am indebted in part for my facts, to the authority of Mr. McCulloch.* The sugar planter always forms a connexion

* Com. Dict. Tit. Colonies.

with a mercantile house in London, Liverpool, Bristol or Glasgow. He usually stipulates for an advance on his crops, usually from £3,000 to £4,000 for every 100 hogsheads of sugar which the plantation can be relied on to produce. To secure these advances, the planter always gives a mortgage, which is renewed from year to year, and binds himself to send his crops to the commission house, allowing it full mercantile commissions. The regular commissions are $2\frac{1}{2}$ per cent. on the amount of sugar sold, and of plantation stores sent out, adding one-half per cent. on all insurance effected.

The sale of West India articles takes place through the medium of produce brokers, who, in London, reside chiefly in Mincing lane and Tower street. Samples of sugar and rum are on show in their respective sale rooms, four days of the week, from 11 to 1 o'clock; during which time the sugar refiners and dealers call, observe the market and make their purchases. The sales are usually made on short credit; one month usually for coffee and rum, and two months for sugar. Coffee is usually sold at auction; sugar and rum at private sale; and all by sample.

The shipment of stores is briefly as follows: The merchant in England receives from the planters, in the autumn of each year, a list of the articles required for the estate or estates upon which he holds his lien; these lists they divide, arrange and distribute among different wholesale

dealers in the course of September and October, with instructions to get them ready to ship in a few weeks. November and December are the chief months for the
despatch of outward-bound West Indiamen, as the plantation stores are usually required by the end of December,
or in all the month of January. The arrivals of West
Indiamen in England with homeward crops, begin in
April, and continue till October. Heavy vessels cannot
well be loaded during the autumnal months.

Since the above was written I have received a letter
from an intelligent gentleman residing in one of the British
North American provinces, who spent many years of his
life in one of the West India islands, previous to the abolition of slavery, and whose testimony in behalf of some
of the views I have expressed has seemed worth quoting.
It will be perceived that he agrees with me in regard to
the insolvent condition of the British West Indies before
the abolition of slavery, and his explanation of the cause
of that insolvency fills a place in my analysis which I could
not more adequately supply, than by copying his letter
entire.

TORONTO, U. C., Sept. 14, 1850.

Dear Sir :—

I have experienced great pleasure during the past season in reading some communications which have appeared
in the *New York Evening Post*, relative to the Island of
Jamaica, and which are attributed to your pen. Your
editorial connexion with that journal tended to confirm the
report, and I write under that impression to assure you,
that though myself a British subject, a residence of
several years in the British West Indies, enables me to
bear testimony to the truthfulness of your statements, and
the soundness of your conclusions.

I was gratified to see that you took proper notice of
the bankrupt condition of the island before slavery was
abolished. That fact deserves all the prominence that can
be given to it. I think, however, you have overlooked one
of the causes of that condition of things, of no secondary
importance. At least I do not remember to have seen it
noticed in any of your communications which have fallen
under my eye, and I hope if you write any more upon the
subject you will give it a share of your attention. I refer
to the restrictions upon the commerce between those islands
and foreign nations which prevailed for many years previous and subsequent to the abolition of slavery.

Those who are acquainted with the West Indies, are
aware that at one time salt fish formed the principle article
of food, with which the planters supplied their slaves ; and
it was for the purpose of encouraging the fisheries of the
North American provinces, that its introduction from the
United States was prohibited. It is true, that the ports

were sometimes thrown open by proclamation of the Governor, as for example when extensive fires took place, and lumber was required to replace the buildings that had been destroyed, or when approaching famine was apparent. But this was of such uncertain occurrence, that no regular trade could be engaged in, from the United States ; and when the exigency had ceased, the ports were again closed as before. It was an assumption of power on the part of the Governors to suspend the operation of an Act of the Imperial Parliament, which rendered an act of indemnity necessary on their retiring from their government ; and consequently they rarely incurred the responsibility of such interference unless when demanded by an urgent necessity.

Such being the situation of the planters, and being compelled to pay on an average double what they should have done for the support of their negroes, it is not surprising that, in the absence of that tact and economy which never co-exist with slavery, they became gradually insolvent, and after a lapse of years, their estates very generally were encumbered. Although the other islands labored under the same disadvantage as to the importation of food, yet it bore with peculiar hardship upon Jamaica, as vessels from the North American provinces first touched at Barbadoes in search of a market, and failing in obtaining one there, ran down the islands, selling where they could ; and if unable to meet with a sale before, bore up for Jamaica as a last resort. The consequence was, either a glut or a scarcity, and no steady or uniform price ever prevailed.

This state of things commenced with the independence of the United States, and it is not to be wondered at, therefore, that the planters were ultimately impoverished. This result was particularly apparent in Jamaica, where the estates for the most part, as you stated very correctly, were eventually mortgaged, or held under execution, which was periodically renewed at considerable expense. The consequence was, that when the British Parliament made the munificent national donation of twenty millions sterling, to remunerate the masters for the loss of their slaves, the most of that immense sum went into the pockets of the creditor in England ; and as the slaves were paid for at a rate far beneath their real value, the amount received was rarely enough to pay off the encumbrances, and when they were, the owner was left with the mere skeleton of his property as it were, and without the means of procuring hired labor.

Owing to the innate indolence of the African, and the ease and facility with which, in a tropical climate, his wants may be supplied, it will readily be admitted that the difficulties and embarrassments of the planter were increased ; but had he not been previously so embarrassed and involved in difficulty, or had he been able to appropriate the amount which he received for his slaves—reduced as it was—in working his estate, the condition of the West India islands would have been very different from what it is at present. Of course there were some exceptions, but generally speaking, as you stated, estates—particularly in the Island of Jamaica—were encumbered for more than their value when the Emancipation Act was passsd, and for the reasons I have stated, have not since been cultivated to advantage.

You will readily perceive that the protective system ma-

terially increased the expense of managing estates, by increasing the price of the necessaries of life ; and yet, as
you have remarked, the West Indians are now clamorous
for similar duties, by which the price of their productions
will be enhanced in the British market, thus entailing privation upon the community which consumes them.

With an immense extent of sea-board abounding with fish,
which the fisherman could take in his boat, and which his
family could daily cure on the shore, they were certainly
in a position advantageously to compete with the American, who, from Cape Cod and Marblehead, found his way
through the Gut of Canso to the Gulf of St. Lawrence
and the Straits of Bell Isle, and who, after salting down
his fish in the hold, had to return with it to his distant
home, and cure it there. Yet with all these obstructions,
the Americans, in consequence of the supineness and inertness of the colonists, could easily have undersold them in
their own markets, had they been allowed to frequent
them.

And, while the West India planter became embarrassed
by the high prices he paid for the necessaries of life, those
whom the protective system was intended to benefit, derived
no advantage from its operation ; fish being at a low rate
at the places whither the fisherman repaired to dispose of
his catch, owing to the uncertainty that attended every
shipment which was made, caused by the frequent and
ruinous fluctuations in the West India market ; while the
merchant, on the other hand, was often ruined by the losing
voyages of his vessels. In fact, the West India trade was
a sort of lottery, in which there were a great many blanks

and ultimately but few prizes. Halifax was at one time the principal shipping port to the West Indies, but I cannot at this moment call to mind the names of half-a-dozen of its merchants who eventually retired gainers by their operations in that trade.

Excuse the length of this communication and the liberty I have taken, of attempting to add to your information upon a subject about which you seem to be so thoroughly informed, and believe me,

Very respectfully,

And truly yours,

EDMUND WARD.

To

JOHN BIGELOW, ESQ.

CHAPTER XI.

Accumulations of land—No middle class—Labor not capital.

I HAVE referred to the insolvent condition of the Jamaicans previous to the emancipation of the slaves, and have shown that even then, the whole business of the island was done upon credit, given upon the most ruinous terms. I have also given my reasons for believing that the Emancipation Act did not cause, but only precipitated a result which was inevitable ; it compelled a balance to be struck between the debtors and the creditors, which revealed, rather than begat, the poverty which now, no effort can conceal.

But the question arises, why have not the properties been sold by the necessitous and purchased upon terms that would admit of careful and remunerating cultivation ; in other words, why have not the laws of supply and demand dispossessed the absentee landlords, converted the mortgagees into resident proprietors, and thus restored the equilibrium between labor and capital ?

This is the Jamaica problem. Without presuming to

be able to give it a scientific solution with the means of information at present within my reach, I think I can indicate the direction in which such a solution is to be found, by those who may choose to go in quest of it.

I have already stated that nine-tenths of the land is owned by non-resident proprietors. That involves the necessity of trusting its culture to agents. The agency for an estate of two hundred acres, costs on an average, not less than for one of a thousand acres, and the larger the estate, therefore, the less the relative expense of its agencies.

Again, it would not be worth while for a non-resident to keep up the supervision of a moderate sized farm, three thousand miles from home. Nothing less than the profits of a very large estate, could compensate him for the trouble and pexense of keeping up a force of attornies, agents and book-keepers, and for the absence of that personal devotion to its management, which none but a proprietor ever feels.

To these and other circumstances, which it is not mateial now to enumerate, may be attributed the tendency which has been active here since the settlement of the island by the English, to accumulate real estate in the hands of large proprietors, and to exterminate from the soil, all men of small capital. Till recently, such a thing was never known as a small farm of fifty or a hundred acres to be put under culture for profit. A place of this description would be called a *pen* here, which is the name by which they designate a country residence, and would be appropriated to kitchen and ornamental gardening, parks and orchards, but would not be reckoned a productive part of the proprietor's estate.

Out of one hundred and forty sugar estates in Jamaica, selected indiscriminately, the average size of each was over 1,202 acres. There is no reason to doubt that the average size throughout the whole island is still greater. For example, eight estates, which have been abandoned in the parish of St. Ann, contained in the aggregate 10,330 acres; one in St. Dorothy, and the only one, contained 1,406; two in St. John, contained 2,960; two in Vere, contained 3,860; seventeen in Clarendon, contained 23,737; in Port Royal, one contained 1,780; in St Davids, two contained 3,662; in St. Elizabeth, six contained 18,010; and in Westmoreland, two contained, 3,889.

Of course, estates like these, can only be owned and cultivated by men of large capital, who are generally unwilling to sell fragments of their property for the reasons I have already suggested. Beside considering it unprofitable to own a small estate, which they have to commit to the expensive management of agents, they have an idea that no money is to be made here except from sugar, rum and coffee, articles which the negroes know how to produce as well as, or better, than the whites. If they attempt anything else, the negroes must learn how to do the work, and the white superintendents are generally too ignorant, too lazy, or too indifferent, to take the trouble to teach them.   To cultivate either of the great staples, it has always been esteemed necessary to have very expensive works attached to each estate, costing generally from ten to forty or fifty thousand pounds.   I have seen sugar works here which cost sixty thousand pounds.   Of course their expense does not increase in proportion to the size of the property; on the contrary, like the expenses of superintendence, it costs but little more for machinery to manufacture the sugar and the rum for an estate of two hundred acres, than for one five times its size.   Hence it is supposed that the value of a large estate, would be impaired by dividing it, and that the larger it is, the greater is its worth per acre.   I shall have occasion to show by-and-by how entirely wrong the planters are in their facts, and in their inferences upon this subject, but it is enough at present for me to state, what will not be disputed, that the whole proprietorship of the island is infected with the impression, that the real estate is valuable in an inverse ratio to the number of proprietors; that the more simple the kind of labor required, the greater will be its product, and that sugar, rum and coffee, can be produced on that account, more profitably than anything else.

Hence it happens that when a proprietor sells a property,

whether from necessity or choice, he insists upon selling the whole of it, and the purchaser generally insists upon buying the whole. The residents of the island are, for the most part, too poor to buy, and hence non-residents have usually been the purchasers, when any sales were made. In this way, all the evils of absenteeism have been perpetuated, and the few sales which have occurred, have contributed nothing, apparently, to the restoration of the equilibrium between labor and capital, which must precede any permanent prosperity in Jamaica.

Another consequence of this delusion about the necessity of preserving the present monstrous proportions of the estates is, that most of the capital invested here is appropriated to the two or three favorite staples which I have mentioned, and the island is compelled to import nearly everything it consumes. It will hardly seem credible, that a country which can grow any kind of grain, almost without culture, should import all its flour, its meal, its rice, and immense quantities of peas and beans for the consumption of its own population; that a country which supports a larger variety of valuable forest trees than any other tract of its size in the world, should import all its lumber, its shingles, its staves, its heading and its hoop poles; that an island which, if left to run wild, would afford better grazing to cattle all the year round, than can be procured at any season in any one of the United States, unless it be

Texas, with cultivation, should import all its smoked and
salt beef, all its salt pork, hams and tongues, most of its
butter, lard, cheese, candles, and soap; and yet incredible
as it may appear, such has been the custom in Jamaica for
years, as the following table which I found in De Cordova's
Mercantile Intelligencer, a very useful paper published
periodically at Kingston, will demonstrate :

*Imports into the Island of Jamaica (Kingston and the
Outports) up to the 10th of October in the years* 1848
and 1849.

	1849.	1848
Flour, bbls	70,634	82,399
Meal, ditto	24,716	21,949
Bread, cwts	6,386	11,280
Rice, lbs	4,587,155	2,944,314
Corn, bushels	87,003	123 133
Peas and Beans, bushels	11,466	13,759
Barley, Oats, and Rye, ditto	1,117	745
Wheat, ditto	10,909	7,867
Beef, bbls	1,741	2,181
Pork, do	17,281	21,176
Wet Tongues, do	417	414
Dry Tongues Beef and Hams } cwts	5,264	2,807
Butter, firkins	14,032	11,677
Lard, do	7,737	7,369
Herrings, boxes	4,590	1,159
Mackerel, do	34,650	30,560
Alewives, do	4,220	3,250
Herrings, do	15,230	15,721
Codfish, quintals	91,439	112,455
Cheese, cwts	1,406	1,866
Refined Sugar, lbs	57,404	43,796
Candles, Sperm, boxes	1,478	677
do Composition, boxes	1,168	1,172
do Tallow, do	11,486	9,250
Soap do	52,706	42,637
Tobacco, manufactured, lbs	253,610	224,497
do leaf do	94,751	309,879

	1849.	1848.
Bricks, number..........................	899,700	929,520
Staves, R O......,......................	967,688	1,336,715
do W. O. and Heading..............	503,653	642,258
Hogshead Shooks........................	1,862	1,876
Puncheon do	818	4,509
Lumber, W. P. feet......................	3,632,274	4,544,766
do P. P. feet......................	448,063	2,021,685
Shingles, Cypress......................	894,700	1,714,215
do . Cedar...........................	3,724,884	4,687,085
Wood Hoops.............................	837,811	1,020,181
Hardwood and other Timbers, feet.......	19,321	8,333

It will be perceived by this table, that the importation
of salt fish is very large, and yet the waters around Jamaica, abound with some of the finest fish in the world.
The people will send to Maine for lumber, and pay $25 a
thousand feet for it, rather than be at the trouble of cutting down their own magnificent forests.   There is not a
single saw mill upon the island.   There are no manufactories of any kind except of sugar and rum.   Even
their brick they import.   The hilly surface of the country
supplies an abundance of water power, over forty constant
rivers and over two hundred rivulets, and yet there is not
such a thing as a water wheel to be found in use, except
on the plantations and for agricultural purposes.

So entirely, indeed, are the capital and industry of the
island absorbed in the culture of favorite staples on these
large estates, that common articles of table consumption
in Kingston, are higher than in any part of England or the
United States.   I give below a list of prices paid at the

hotel where I stayed, for articles, every one of which could be cultivated in Jamaica with the utmost ease and abundance, and ought to be sold for prices far below the current rates for the same articles in any city in the United States:

Butter, per lb.,	37½
Cow's milk, per quart,	18¾
Goat's milk, per quart,	25
American cheese, per lb.,	25
English cheese, per lb.,	37½
Potatoes, per lb.,	6¼
Eggs, 2 for	6¼
" during the Christmas holidays 5 cents a piece.	
Garlick, per lb.,	25 a 37¼
Flour, per lb.,	12 a 18
do per barrel,	$16 a $18
Corn meal, per bbl.,	$12 a $14
Hams, at retail, per lb.,	25
Lard, per lb.,	21
Onions, per lb.,	12½

Nothing apparently can be more unnatural, than for the people of this island, in their present poverty-stricken condition, to be paying such prices as these for their daily food; and yet nothing is more inevitable, so long as the land is held by a few absentee landlords, in such large quantities.

No one who has lived in a slave country need be told that it never supports a middle class. The intelligent white operative with no capital but his muscles, his character, and his ambition, will never settle in a country where all muscular labor is performed by a degraded caste. Where slavery exists, there are but two classes, the capitalist and the slave. The union of capital and labor in the same person never occurs. The consequence is, that in Jamaica where the moral influence of slavery yet abides, there are none of those small proprietors, so common throughout the northern part of the United States, who, with the savings from their daily wages, buy a few acres of land, which they cultivate with their own hands, enlarging from time to time as convenience will permit, and on which they raise a large proportion of the articles required for their family consumption. Had Jamaica such a population, we would never hear again of her importing annually seventy thousand barrels of flour, ninety thousand bushels of corn, three hundred thousand pounds of tobacco, ten or twelve million feet of lumber and sawed stuff; her population would not have to pay thirty-eight cents a pound for butter, eighteen cents a quart for milk, three to five cents a piece for eggs, twenty-five cents a pound for ham, and sixteen to eighteen dollars for a barrel of flour. But as I have before stated, slavery and absenteeism together, have distributed the land in princely tracts to large capitalists, whose interest has always been supposed to be best consulted, by cultivating two or three leading staples, to the general neglect of all articles of home consumption, and by whom the multiplication of small land proprietors has never been favored. It is not surprising, therefore, that even in this country, favored with a climate and soil which almost supplies the wants of man, spontaneously, it costs quite as much to live as in the most expensive cities of the United States.

CHAPTER XII.

I HAVE with all practicable brevity stated what I look upon as the more prominent causes of the present prostrate condition of this charming island. I take leave to re-capitulate them.

First.—The degradation of labor, in consequence of the yet comparatively recent existence of negro slavery, by which the white population are excluded from almost every department of productive industry, and a tone of public opinion is begotten, calculated to discourage, rather than to promote industry among the people of color.

Second.—Nine-tenths of the improved land was owned by absentees—which implies unskilful tillage ; an extra expense on an average of three thousand dollars a year to each estate for attorneys, agents and overseers ; great im-providence in the management of the properties, and few or no labor-saving improvements.

Third.—The estates under culture were all mortgaged

for more than they were worth, when the emancipation bill passed. That measure increased the embarrassments of the residents, made them the easy prey of their non-resident creditors, and left them without means or capital to conduct the cultivation of the land with profit or even with economy.

Fourth.—The magnitude of the estates and the principles upon which they have been cultivated, prevent the free circulation of real property, tend to accumulate the land in the hands of a few, to exterminate the middle classes of men with little or no capital, and to beget a constant and unnatural antagonism between capital and labor.

These causes, in my judgment, would have conducted Jamaica to inevitable ruin, had the tariff laws never been altered nor the slaves been set at liberty.

But the question arises, is this state of things to be perpetual, or where or how is it to terminate? I answer, that it must continue until the land gets into the hands of people who are not ashamed to till it. So long as it is held by English landlords, it will doubtless continue to depreciate in value. I say this with all possible respect for the proprietary class here, many of whom I know, and greatly esteem. It will continue to depreciate in their hands, I say, because they will not cultivate it personally, nor can they command the capital, fidelity and skill necessary to cultivate it with profit by agents. It will continue to depreciate until the landholders will consent to sell small fragments of their estates to the poorer classes who are willing to work the land with their own hands.

The island proprietors cannot command the capital nor the skill necessary to cultivate their large estates profitably now, whatever they might have done in more prosperous times, and before they became so poor and involved. They are realizing this more and more distinctly every day. The market value of course must go on declining as long as the present proportions of the estates are preserved, until the lower prices tempt labor and small capitalists from abroad, or until the land comes within the reach of the poorer classes of the colored population. That point has been nearly reached. There has been as yet but little movement toward the island from abroad, because its actual condition and resources are not correctly understood in other countries, especially among the class most likely to avail themselves of a new field of enterprise on a foreign soil. But the colored residents have already discovered their advantage, and are availing themselves, in considerable numbers, of the cheapness of real estate, to become proprietors.

I was surprised to find how general was the desire among the negroes to become possessed of a little land, and upon what sound principles that desire was based. In the first place, a freehold of four or five acres gives them a vote, to which they attach great value, and in the next place, it enables them with two or three months of labor upon wages during the cropping of the sugar, and one day in each week devoted to their little farms, to live in comparative ease and independence. From five acres of land in Jamaica, a negro will supply almost all his physical wants. I have seen growing on a patch of less than two acres, owned by a negro, the bread fruit, bananas, yams, oranges, shadducks, cucumbers, beans, pine-apple, plantain and chiramoya, besides many kinds of shrubbery and fruits of secondary value.

I was greatly surprised to find that the number of these colored proprietors is already considerably over one hundred thousand, and constantly increasing.

When one reflects that only sixteen years ago there was scarcely a colored land-holder upon the island, and that now there are a hundred thousand, it is unnecessary to say that this class of the population appreciate the privileges of free labor and a homestead far more correctly than might be expected, more especially when it is borne in mind that seven-tenths of them were begotten in slavery, and spent many years of their lives as bondsmen.

Their properties average I should think, about three acres. They have a direct interest in cultivating them economically and intelligently. The practice of planning their own labor, encouraged by the privilege of reaping its rewards themselves, exerts upon them the most important educational influence, the results of which will soon be much more apparent than they are now.

Upon their little tracts they raise not only what they require for their own consumption, but a surplus which they take to market, usually in small panniers upon donkies, or upon their heads. Nearly every colored proprietor has a donkey, which costs from seven to ten pounds, upon which he packs his produce, and under the custody sometimes of a woman, often of a child, he sends it to town, to be converted into money, with which he purchases such articles of necessity or luxury as his land does not produce and he can afford. One of the most interesting spectacles to be witnessed about Kingston, is presented on the highroad through which the market people, with their donkies, in the cool of the morning, pour into the city from the back country. They form an almost uninterrupted procession four or five miles in length; and what strikes the eye of an American at once, is their perfect freedom from care. Neither anxiety, nor poverty, nor desire of gain, has written a line upon their faces, and they could not show less concern at the result of their trip if they were going to a festival. One may readily perceive how strong and universal must be the desire of the poor laborers to exchange their servile drudgery, on the lands of others, for this life of comparative ease and independence.

Of course it requires no little self-denial and energy for a negro, upon the wages now paid in Jamaica, to lay up enough with which to purchase one of these properties, but if he does get one, he never parts with it, except for a larger or a better one. The planters call them lazy for indulging in this feeling of independence ; but I never could see anything in the aversion of the negroes here to labor, which was not sanctioned by the example of their masters, and by instincts and propensities common to humanity.

The planters discourage these sales of land to the blacks in every possible way, for they say it raises the price of labor by increasing the independence of the laboring classes. They insist that a negro will not work longer than he is obliged to, for the mere supply of the necessaries of life, which are very few and very cheap. They say with Carlyle, that " where a black man by working about half an hour a day (such is the calculation,) can supply himself, by aid of sun and soil, with as much pumpkin as will suffice, he is likely to be a little stiff to raise into hard work ! Supply and demand, which, science says, should be brought to bear on him, have an up-hill task of it with such a man. Strong sun supplies itself gratis, rich soil in those unpeopled or half-peopled regions almost gratis ; these are *his* ' supply ; ' and half an hour a day, directed upon these, will produce pumpkin, which is his ' demand.' The fortunate black man, very swiftly does he settle *his* account with supply and demand :—not so swiftly the less

fortunate white man of these tropical localities. He himself cannot work; and his black neighbor, rich in pumpkin,
is in no haste to help him. Sunk to the ears in pumpkin,
imbibing saccharine juices, and much at his ease in the
Creation, he can listen to the less fortunate white man's
' demand,' and take his own time in supplying it. Higher
wages, massa; higher, for your cane-crop cannot wait;
still higher,—till no conceivable opulence of cane-crop
will cover such wages !"

The estimate put upon voluntary black labor in the
above extract by Mr. Carlyle, is quite generally entertained
among the planters in Jamaica, and among the slaveholders in the United States, and as it is entirely inconsistent with my own, it is proper that I should give the result
of my observations of free negro labor here, and the extent
to which I have found it governed by the laws which
generally are found to control other kinds of labor.
Before doing so, however, I wish to say a word of the
communication from which the above extract is made.

It is difficult for one who is acquainted with his earlier
writings, to believe that the "Occasional Discourse on
Negro Slavery," to which I have referred, is from the pen
of Carlyle. It lacks all the moral, and many of the intellectual traits which have distinguished the writings of
that gifted man. The argument of the discourse is briefly
as follows. The negro has few wants, and those almost

exclusively of an animal nature, which he can and does supply with very little labor. He will not work more than is necessary to supply those wants, without receiving exorbitant wages. But it is a law of our nature, says the writer, "that no black man who shall not work according to what ability the gods have given him for working, has the smallest right to eat pumpkin or to any fraction of land that will grow pumpkin, however plentiful such land may be; but has an indisputable and perpetual *right* to be compelled, by the real proprietors of said land, to do competent work for his living. That is the everlasting duty of all men, white or black, who are born into the world."

Mr. Carlyle proceeds to claim that pumpkins are not "the sole pre-requisites for human well-being." Many other things grow among these islands useful to man, such as sugar, coffee, cinnamon, and precious spices, "things far nobler than pumpkins; and leading towards commerces, arts, politics and social developments, which alone are the noble product, where men (and not pigs with pumpkins) are the parties concerned! * * * * "If Quashee will not honestly aid in bringing out those sugars, cinnamons, and nobler products of the West Indian islands, for the benefit of all mankind, then I say neither will the Powers permit Quashee to continue growing pumpkins there for his own lazy benefit; but will sheer him out, by-and-by, like a lazy gourd overshadowing rich

ground ; him and all that partake with him,—perhaps in
a very terrible manner. For, under favor of Exeter Hall,
the 'terrible manner' is not yet quite extinct with the
Destinies in this Universe ; nor will it quite cease, I apprehend, for soft sawder or philanthropic stump-oratory now
or henceforth. No ; the gods wish besides pumpkins, that
spices and valuable products be grown in their West
Indies ; thus much they have so declared in making the
West Indies :—infinitely more they wish, that manful industrious men occupy their West Indies, not indolent two-
legged cattle, however 'happy' over their abundant pumpkins ! Both these thing, we may be assured, the immortal
gods have decided upon, passed their eternal act of parliament for : and both of them, though all terrestrial Parlia-
ments and entities oppose it to the death, shall be done,
Quashee, if he will not help in bringing out the spices,
will get himself made a slave again (which state will be a
little less ugly than his present one), and with beneficent
whip, since other methods avail not, will be compelled to
work.   *   *   *   *   *   *   *
You are not 'slaves' now ; nor do I wish, if it can be
avoided, to see you slaves again : but decidedly you will
have to be servants to those that are born *wiser* than
you, that are born lords of you,—servants to the whites,
if they *are*, as what mortal can doubt they are? born
wiser than you. That you may depend upon it my ob-

scure Black friends, is and was always the Law of the World, for you and for all men : To *be* servants, the more foolish of us to the more wise ; and only sorrow, futility and disappointment will betide both, till both in some approximate degree get to conform to the same. Heaven's laws are not repealable by Earth, however Earth may try,—and it has been trying hard, in some directions, of life ! I say, no well-being and in the end no being at all, will be possible for you or us, if the law of Heaven is not complied with. And if 'slave' mean essentially 'servant hired for life,'—for life, or by a contract of long continuance and not easily dissoluble,—I ask, whether, in all human things, the 'contract of long continuance' is not precisely the contract to be desired, were the right terms once found for it ? Servant hired for life, were the right terms once found, which I do not pretend they are, seems to me much preferable to servant hired for the month, or by contract dissoluble in a day. An ill-situated servant, that ;—servant grown to be *nomadic ;* between whom and his master a good relation *cannot* easily spring up !"

Such is the solution of the West Indian problem, advocated by one of the most distinguished writers and thinkers in England : a restoration of slavery. He would introduce compulsory labor, the price of which should not be regulated by the laws of supply and demand which control the wages of whites, but by acts of parliament, or by the caprice and avarice of land-owners. If this form of slavery should not be effectual, he would restore the chattel slavery which formerly prevailed. He admits that the whites do not work here, but he does not propose to make labor compulsory upon them. He would have the rate of wages for the negroes determined by an arbitrary regulation and not by the supply, as it is everywhere else. He would exclude all white laborers from the West Indies, by compelling the blacks to work at lower than market prices.

As these propositions logically assume that the organization of the black man is inferior to that of the white man—and that he is not entitled to equal rights before the law, but is to be classified with the brute creation, I have no occasion to notice them farther than to state them, for I am sure that there are but few of my readers who would be interested in the discussion of such enormities. But as Mr. Carlyle farther justifies the course he recommends, by the allegation that the negroes will not work after their animal wants are supplied, and as such a statement, if true, is calculated to destroy all hope of ever bringing the blacks within the pale of an exalted civilization, I desire a word with my readers upon that point.

CHAPTER XIII.

Labor and Wages.

THE complaint made by Mr. Carlyle, is the first thing which a stranger hears out of the mouths of white residents on landing at Jamaica. "The wages are so high that nothing can be made off our estates without protection." They clamor from the house tops that there is a scarcity of labor, which causes the high wages; and the island is constantly agitated with schemes for the importation of laborers from abroad. Coolies were brought here many years ago from the East; the Apprenticeship system was established; immigration from Germany and Africa was encouraged at some expense, but still the complaint is, that wages are ruinously high. I did not meet a single planter, who did not insist that it was the unnatural price of labor that was sinking them. Mr. Stanley carried off the same impression, and makes it the staple of his argument for a restoration of the old protective duties on colonial produce.

Now it never seems to have occurred either to Mr. Stanley or to Mr. Carlyle, that their readers might feel an interest in knowing what the enormous wages were, which failed to overcome the indolence of the "pumpkin eating, two legged cattle," who compose the operative classes in the West Indies. As information upon this point seemed to be of the very last importance in determining whether there was a scarcity of labor, or certain constitutional infirmities in the laborers to overcome, which created a necessity for special legislation, I made the current wages of the island the subject of special inquiry. To my utter surprise I learned, that the price for men on the sugar and coffee plantations ranged from eighteen to twenty-four cents a day, and proportionably less for boys and females. Out of these wages, the laborers have *to board themselves*. Now when it is considered that in the largest market on the island, flour costs from sixteen to eighteen dollars by the barrel, butter thirty-eight cents a pound, eggs from three to five cents a piece, and hams twenty-five cents a pound; does not the cry of high wages appear absurd? Was the wolf's complaint of the lamb for muddying the water in the stream below him, more unreasonable? Are wages lower in any quarter of the civilized world? Four-fifths of all the grain consumed in Jamaica is grown in the United States, on fields where labor costs more than four times this price, and where every kind of provision, but fruit, is less expensive. The fact is, the negro cannot live on such wages, unless he owns in fee, a lot of three or five acres, or ekes them out by stealing. He is driven by necessity to the purchase and cultivation of land for himself, and he finds such labor, so much better rewarded than that bestowed upon the lands of others, that he very naturally takes care of his own first, and gives his leisure to the properties of others, when he feels inclined; in that particular acting very much as if he were a white man.

But far better evidence than the nominal cost of labor, may be produced to show that wages are actually very low. In the first place, every house and shop is filled with black servants. People with incomes of less than five hundred dollars a year, will keep more servants than would be expected in the United States, from an annual income of ten thousand.

When the census was taken in 1844, it appeared that there were in Jamaica at that time 23,153 household servants, under which name I do not mean to include agricultural or day laborers of any kind, who number about 200,000 more. By the same census it appeared, that there were 142,831 persons without any occupation or pursuit. Here we have over 160,000 persons, or more than 2-5ths of the whole population, unproductive, comparatively.

There are from three to five times as many persons employed about everything as are necessary. The most modest and economical establishment in the country, will have four or five domestic servants. Field hands are multiplied until they are in each others way, and the amplest provision is always made to prevent the possibility of the ruling race, being compelled to do anything themselves, which can be done by servants.

I was particularly struck with the absurdity of this complaint about the high price of labor one day, when I was on a visit to a delightful sugar estate, lying in the parish of St. Thomas in the Vale. It was formerly the property of Bryan Edwards, whose excellent history of the British West Indies is well known in the United States.*

Dove Hall, for that is the name of the estate, lies near

* Bryan Edwards was born in Westbury, Eng., County of Wilts, in 1743. His mother had two opulent brothers in Jamaica, one of whom—Zachary Bailey—took the family under his protection upon the death of the father. Bryan was educated in England, and at an early age settled in Jamaica. He was for a long time a member of the Assembly, and was also a member of the British Parliament. In 1793 he published his History, Civil and Commercial, of the British Colonies in the West Indies, in three octavo volumes, by far the best work in every point of view, that has been written about those islands. He was perfectly informed about his subject, truthful and moderate in his statements, as free from prejudice as any man of sensibility could be, and perfectly indefatigable in his preparation. He is sometimes a little garrulous, and frequently neglected opportunities of condensing, which he might have taken advantage of, profitably; but with every allowance for such imperfections, to this history the inquirer must still turn to inform himself of the historical origin and physical resources of the British West Indies. Edwards died long before the abolition of slavery—about 1800 I believe. Of course, therefore, we have none of his observations upon the effect of that measure upon the colonies, but in the course of his history he frequently alludes to the evil of slavery—he was himself a large slaveholder—and regrets that there seemed to be no possibility of getting rid of the institution without doing more harm than good.

the base of a mountain, beautifully wooded with the most
luxuriant forest trees of the tropics.   The mansion is upon
an elevation which gradually slopes, for near a quarter of
a mile, till it is bounded in the valley by extensive fields of
sugar cane, which skirt the margin of a beautiful river that
traverses the whole estate.   As I drove into the lawn in
front of the house, I observed from fifty to seventy-five
head of cattle—oxen, cows, and donkeys—grazing about,
and three men and two boys, posted at different points,
were watching them, occasionally varying the monotony of
their duties by rolling over on the grass and chattering to
each other, *de rebus nihili*, in that peculiarly rapid and
thoughtless gibberish which one never hears, except from
negroes and monkeys.

When I entered the house, I asked what these negroes
were doing on the lawn, and was told that they were tend-
ing the cattle to keep them from wandering off into the
mountain.   Before I left, the overseer of the estate assured
me in all sincerity, that the planters could not get ahead
in Jamaica unless wages came down ?   I told him that he
must not talk to an American about high wages, when he
could afford to keep three men and two boys to do what
was not more than half occupation for the smallest of the
boys.*

---

* My readers will probably share the surprise which I experienced when I read
the statement about wages which occurs in the following passage in Mr. Stanley's

This is but one of the thousand ways in which labor is squandered on this island. In the sugar mills, from twenty to thirty men and women will be employed to do what five American operatives would do much better in the same time, with the aid of such labor-saving agencies as would suggest themselves at once to an intelligent mind. Everything is done in a way rather to increase than diminish the number of hands required. I venture to say, that there is not one single step in the manufacture of a hogshead of sugar, or a puncheon of rum, upon any estate in Jamaica, in which any intelligent mechanic might not point out a palpable waste of labor, and a ready process of saving it.

I could not learn that there were any estates on the island, decently stocked with implements of husbandry. Even the modern axe is not in general use ; for felling the larger class of trees, the negroes commonly use what they call an axe, which is shaped much like a wedge, except that it is a little wider at the edge than at the opposite end, at the very extremity of which, a perfectly straight han-

letter to Mr. Gladstone :—" Of course it is easy and plausible to assert, that no man works so well as when working for his own profit—that the hope of raising himself in the social scale is among the strongest incentives by which the human mind can be actuated—and to point to the English or American laborer as a proof of a somewhat hastily drawn conclusion. But in practice it has invariably been found, that so far from having advanced since the days of the apprenticeship, the negro laborer has on the whole retrograded (vide Lord Grey's despatch, quoted above); that indolence, not industry, has been the result of his freedom ; that the task performed by him is not one half of what his strength would enable him to accomplish in an easy day's work ; and that for this service, such as it is, he demands A PRICE WHICH WOULD BE DEEMED EXORBITANT IN ANY OTHER PART OF THE WORLD."

dle is inserted.   A more awkward thing for chopping could
not be well conceived—at least so I thought until I saw
the instrument in yet more general use about the houses
in the country, for cutting fire-wood.   It was in shape,
size and appearance, more like the outer half of the blade
of a scythe, stuck into a small wooden handle, than anything else I can compare it to ; with this long knife, for it
is nothing else, I have seen negroes hacking at branches of
palm for several minutes, to accomplish what a good
wood-chopper, with an American axe, would finish at a
single stroke.   I am not now speaking of the poorer class
of negro proprietors, whose poverty or ignorance might excuse this, but of the proprietors of large estates, which
have cost their thousands of pounds.

During my stay in Jamaica an address was delivered to
the people of Kingston, by Mr. W. W. Anderson, a very
respectable and much esteemed lawyer of that city, who
has travelled extensively in the United States, and who
took occasion to contrast the industrial policy of the two
countries, with the view of showing to his fellow citizens
the real cause of their declining prosperity.   He noticed
particularly their neglect to avail themselves of the improvements making in every department of agricultural
industry.   Being a resident, and addressing his fellow
citizens, his opinions upon these subjects are worth re-
peating.

"Certainly," says Mr. Anderson, "their (the Americans) superiority over us is not to be found either in their soil or climate, but in their more laboriously and more skilfully directed industry, aided by implemental husbandry. If an acre is to be planted in corn or potatoes, the usual course for a Jamaica farmer is to send twelve or fifteen laborers with their hoes, and probably at the end of the day the ground may have been turned up. And then follows the planting, which is done slowly by the hand, and the making of the drills, and subsequently the cleaning and moulding are all accomplished by the tedious and primitive process of hand-hoeing.

"But in America how is it? A single man, with his little one-horse plough, is sent to the field alone, and in a day he does the work of fifteen of ours. Then the harrowing follows with equal speed, facility and economy of labor; and sowing by a machine which does by an almost simultaneous operation the three-fold work of making a drill, dropping the seed at equal distances, and covering it up—all as quickly as a horse can walk from end to end of the field. As fast as he walks this three-fold work is done by a self-acting machine, which only requires to be dragged over the ground to put the whole of its powers into effective operation. What wonder then at the cheapness of their corn and pork, and the impossibility of our competing with them in these articles so long as we continue in our old ways. We all suffer because, in truth, our neglected rural population is willing to remain a century behind the rest of the world, wedded to their old customs and modes of working—self-satisfied and deficient in enter

prise : and as yet there has been no apostle of a better
system to stir them up.

"The plough is still comparatively rare in this island,
By the cultivators of corn and provisions it is never used,
while it is universal in America.   Were the labor on our
magnificent soils managed by as wise a community, the
increase in the value of our land would be astonishing·
Our land is so cheap and valueless, only because we have
not a system of general cultivation to turn it to profitable
account.   Following our system, America would be poor as
we are.   In their northern states the land is poor and cold,
and yields in most cases little surplus beyond a living, even
after the exertion of such labor, directed by skill and well-
made instruments.   But consider our soil.   See what an
ignorant mountain-cultivator can extract from a single acre.
Seldom, indeed, is it that much is cultivated by a Jamaica
peasant to supply his family's wants.   The abundant and
varied products of the soil enable him to live in comfort
even with so small a modicum of exertion.   Were any man
to work his ten hours a day, and be aided by suitable implements for economizing labor, and better information,
how easily could he achieve for himself comfort and independence."

During the past summer public meetings have been held,
and a vast deal of discussion has taken place in the journals
of the island about the scarcity of labor, with a view of
supporting the statements made by Mr. Stanley, in behalf
of a more liberal protective tariff, and also to induce
Parliament to lend its aid to the encouragement of

foreign immigration. Among the communications to which the controversy has given rise, is the following, addressed by Mr. Anderson, the gentleman last quoted, to the *Colonial Standard*, in explanation of some remarks he had then recently made at a public meeting in Kingston. As local evidence in confirmation of the views I have taken, it has seemed to be entitled to a place in these pages.

" Dear Sir :—

" Let me reply to your observation on the opinions I expressed at the late Cotton meeting about the alleged want of labor, which you say is general throughout the island. I still complain of that statement, and agree with Sir Joshua Rowe* in designating the frequent reiteration of it as absolutely ' suicidal.' It discourages all approach to us of capitalists, and puts a seal on the permanency of depression. I do not say that there is no ground for much complaint; but I say that the extent of the evil, the causes of it, and the remedies for the cure are neither correctly nor

* As Sir Joshua Rowe is Chief Justice of Jamaica, and withal a man whose opinion is deservedly respected here, I will give the remarks to which Mr Anderson refers, as I find them reported in the Colonial Standard :—" Sir Joshua Rowe said that as no other gentlemen present appeared desirous of addressing the meeting, he would, with their permission, make a few observations on the question which they had met to discuss. He agreed with Mr. Wemyss Anderson in the remarks he had made with respect to the quantity of available labor. He had heard a great deal, and read a great deal, about the scarcity of labor, but from all his experience he was inclined, with Mr. Anderson, to the belief that the scarcity was purely local He believed also that the amount of labor varied very materially, even in the same district, and was dependant in a great measure on the manager, for he had found frequently that while one estate was provided with abundant labor, a neighboring estate could not procure a single one. Thnt, however, was not the question they had to consider." &c., &c.

judiciously stated. I of course give those who differ from
me credit for what I thank you for conceding to me, all
honesty in their views and statements. A little discussion
may perhaps elicit something that will prove correcting to
both. What other object, indeed, than the general wel-
fare, can any of us have in our discussions ?

   " The field of my operations for some years past has lain
about six miles from town, and the labor required on it is
hard, consisting chiefly of trenching, ditching, draining of
lagoon lands, and grass planting. I obtain such people
readily, and to any extent for a shilling a day. On my
own small property in the mountains, in the Highgate District, I have also been able to procure laborers with equal
facility at the same rate. Any disappointments that have
occurred, have been trivial. Very much indeed has always depended on these in the management at the time.
My experience, as you truly say, is not very extensive, but
still where such strong general statements are frequently
repeated, it is something in the way of qualification.

   " Again, I can truly say that many individuals in various districts confirm my experience by their own. There
have been, owing to the distresses of the times, many cases
of irregularity in the payments ; and the rate of wages, it
must be admitted, has not afforded much inducement to
cheerful and steady labor in a climate which much encourages languor and indolence. Besides the activity and
strength of mind which education and proper training and
good habits give, is sadly wanting, while the climate much
more than ordinary northern climates, requires all that these
aids can give, to preserve the people from sinking into apa-

thy and vice. Of this aid we all personally feel the importance, but they unfortunately have had but little of it.

" The remedy which has hitherto been relied on, and which you still seem to rely on, is the importation of fresh cargoes of Africans. This I say, and do repeat, as I have often done in my place in the House of Assembly, never can afford any permanent remedy. Social evils will be created by it, if persisted in, of a kind and a magnitude that will fill every one with a surprise and dismay, and in the end utterly destroy our prosperity. We have sought to impart a certain quantity of physical power, while we have abundance of it already lying by us, idle and unemployed. A clergyman told me the other day that the people around him were generally idle, with the exception of an hour or two a day on their grounds. Why not try to make the labor we have available ? The moral incubus of ignorance and immorality must soon affect the fresh importation, as they have our own people. The magnitude of the evils I complain of, will soon become palpable to the most inconsiderate ; while to all thoughtful men the present apprehension of the ultimate consequences to the country must be very serious.

" I blame very much in the matter, the clergy who are the feed guardians and overseers of the morals and education of our peasantry, and ought to be the leaders of their opinions. With a few exceptions, however, they do not generally labor amongst them. The stated canonical preaching amounts, as respects results on an ignorant peasantry, to nothing—and the man who can only show that, as his title to his stipend, ought not to receive it.

The clergy ought to labor on their high vocations as correctly and laboriously, and with the same devotion of time, as the laity do theirs. I am no favorer of Roman Catholic religion, but I confess that the entireness of the devotion of their clergy to their people, excites in me great admiration and respect, and contrasts most unfavorably with all the supineness of a large number of ours. I know not how it is, that with all the avowed checks of bishop, archdeacons, commissaries, vicars, &c., &c., so much usefulness should remain from year to year neglected. We are entitled to look to the clergy for some account of the low condition of our people mentally, socially, and religiously, and of the utter falling to pieces of the social fabric under their charge. There ought to be a Mixed Court, consisting of lay as well as clerical members to look after the whole subject of public instruction, and those who minister to it. Power has never been safe in the hands of ecclesiastics alone : they must not without aid govern each other.

" Sir Charles Lyell, in his valuable book on America, states, that in Massachusetts where education is diffused in abundance throughout the whole body of the people, the labor done in their trades and other avocations, by those whose province it is to labor, is excessive. The truth is, a civilized man, in a well-constituted society, will exert himself almost to death, rather than fail in securing for himself and his family the comforts and the decencies demanded by the habits of the society in which he lives. What amount of fatigue and suffering are not many educated men amongst ourselves now enduring to uphold the decencies and comforts of life to their families ! The higher the pitch to which the mind is wound up by education and moral training, the greater and more self-denying and more energetic will be the efforts to discharge well the duties of life in the social relations.

" Our laboring people are so low and unfeeling in their habits, that they are almost as independent of us as the animals that roam about. We have contentedly witnessed their gradual deterioration, and we do not bestir ourselves to arrest it. We shall never by mere importations of people from Africa, raise the country to true prosperity. That is not the true remedy—quantity we have already, but a good quality of people we have yet to seek, and we must establish it, by every means in our power. The annual grant for education ought not to be less than £5,000.

" I remain, dear sir,
" Yours truly,
" WM. WEMYSS ANDERSON.
" *Richmond Pen, Sept.* 9, 1850."

For these reasons, I submit that the argument by which Messrs. Carlyle and Stanley attempt to justify the interference of Parliament, either to enforce labor or to reward its product by discriminating taxation, is like the facts upon which it rests, without any foundation. The entire neglect of all the most obvious methods of economizing labor, the number of idlers that throng the country, the low wages that are offered, and the utter recklessness with which labor is squandered, fully establish the truth of my statement, that labor in Jamaica is both cheap and abundant. Let labor be rewarded as it is in the United States or even in England, and let it be used with the same economy, and the face of Jamaica would change, almost as rapidly as if the sun of heaven were then to rise upon it for the first time.

CHAPTER XIV

Central Mills.

I HAVE stated that the planters discourage the partition of the land into small properties, because it tends to promote the independence of the laboring classes, and indirectly to advance the cost of labor; I have also stated the prices of labor to range as low as the lowest, in any civilized country in the world, and four or five times lower than in the country from which they import about three-fifths of their bread stuffs. That the apprehensions of the planters are well founded, there can be no question; and that the prices of labor ought to advance, is also beyond a question. Labor will always bring its value unless in some way coerced, and hence its price in Jamaica must rise, or it will continue to be as it now is, inefficient, and its supply irregular. Nor is it the duty of the political economist or the statesman to make it otherwise. It is rather their duty to remove all the restrictions by which it is burdened, and then it will be as abundant and as productive here as it is in countries where it meets with its reward.   Let the law-givers and the capitalists remove all vexatious obstacles to the sale and partition of land, and to the culture of such produce as the island itself has a constant demand for ; let the labor of the negro be converted into capital by furnishing him a home market, for the little surplus which he can raise upon such tracts of land as he can hire and cultivate himself, and labor would rise in price, it is true, but it would rise more in value, for it would be more regular and more productive.   And then land would rise in value also, *pari passu,* for it could be made productive also.   The planter would soon be indemnified either by an increase of his rents or his crops, and the equilibrium of labor and capital, the necessary antecedent to prosperity here as everywhere else, would be restored.

But it is objected by the planting interest, that if the states are so minutely subdivided, the cultivation of the great staples, sugar and coffee, and the manufacture of rum, must cease, because the works upon sugar and coffee estates are very expensive, and require large capital, and the estates must be very large to compensate for the outlay in that direction.   For example, a good range of sugar works could not be erected for less than $50,000.   The proprietor of twenty-five or fifty acres could not afford to keep such costly buildings for the manufacture of his limited stock, much less could the smaller proprietor of three, five or ten acres.

The answer to this objection seems perfectly obvious, and yet no one here seems to understand it. They have only to observe one of the most familiar principles of economical science, and the whole difficulty is obviated. Let them do what is done universally in the northern States of our republic—separate the functions of the agriculturist from those of the manufacturer—and then both departments of industry will be better conducted, upon at least one-tenth the capital now required. There is no conceivable reason why central sugar mills, for example, should not be established, where the planters could take their cane to be ground for a toll, or to sell for a return of a given quantity of sugar, or molasses, or rum, or money, or whatever might be agreed upon. The period for cropping sugar sometimes lasts four months and upwards. The cane can be converted into sugar in less than twelve hours. It is perfectly practicable, therefore, to separate these departments of industry to the profit of both.

Under the system which now prevails here, a planter is usually from three to five months " about," as they term it, that is cutting his cane and making his sugar. He starts his mill in the morning about eight o'clock, and usually stops by five in the afternoon, lets his fires go out and his men go home. Thus the use of more than half his capital is wasted for the period he may have occasion to use his works, and for the balance of the year he loses the use of it altogether. If, on the other hand, the proprietor of a sugar mill were to proclaim a table of rates at which he would make sugar, and also the prices at which he would buy cane, and if he would provide himself with a double set of operatives, who would run his works night and day, never permitting them to stop except on the Sabbath, from the commencement of the sugar harvest to its close, he would save the interest upon the capital invested in them, for all the additional time they were in motion, which would be more than half.

He might also, during the balance of the year, use his engine and buildings in sawing lumber, or in some kind of manufacturing to which they might be adapted, and escape the absurd expense of importing shingles and staves from Maine, lumber from Georgia, refined sugar from Louisiana, and flour and cheese from New York, and all his textile fabrics from Great Britain. By this process, too, the small proprietor might save all his interest upon works and machinery, which constitute such a burden at present to the sugar makers, and by virtue of all the reasons upon which is based the great and familiar principle, that cheap prices follow the division of labor, he would get his canes ground upon better terms than even the large proprietors can do it for themselves, under the present system.

Mr. Stanley very flippantly dismissed from his consideration, this proposal to separate the culture from the manufacture of sugar as one that could only be contended for by men having no practical knowledge of West Indian habits. In his letter to Mr. Gladstone, he says :—

" Again, we are told a great deal of the marvels to be worked at some future period by the negro proprietors or tenants, laboring on their own farms. I have heard it seriously contended, though of course only by men having no practical knowledge of West Indian habits, that this class, having few, if any expenses, and little or nothing to pay in the shape of rent, being moreover capable of endur- ing all the year through, a degree of fatigue which would kill an European in a week, ought to undersell both slave- owners and white employers of free labor. Now on this head I have only a few words to say in answer. First, the business of a sugar estate is two fold : it is an union of agriculture and manufacture. For the latter, at least, skill and combination are required ; of which the negro pos- sesses neither. Nor can this part ot the process be carried on separately from the other ; for the canes, if not taken at once to the mill, are spoilt. On this single ground, the difficulty of carrying on cane cultivation, except on large estates, is almost insuperable—small farming is out of the question. In the next place, appeal to experience—how much sugar has ever been grown for export by the negro farmers ? I will undertake to say, not five tons in any single year, taking the range of all the British islands. And, lastly, the extracts which I have already quoted from official reports and despatches, show sufficiently the estima- tion in which this class is held by those best acquainted

with his character; and consequently the extreme impro-
bability of their succeeding as cultivators of the soil. I
contend then, that the British planter cannot compete in
an English market with the slave owner : that this ina-
bility extends equally to the production of all articles of
export ; and that where the white proprietor has failed, the
negro will not succeed, more especially if, deprived of the
instruction and example of Europeans, by their gradual
abandonment of the island, he is left to retrograde, as there
is but little doubt that he will do, into his pristine condition of African barbarism."

Whether the manufacturing department on a sugar
plantation requires " more skill and power of combination
than the negroes possess," is a question that I need not
stop to discuss. It is enough to answer, that full nine-
tenths of the sugar produced here and in the United States
are manufactured by negroes, with such skill and power of
combination. I may add, that a large number of very
extensive cotton mills are in successful operation in the
States of Georgia, Alabama and Tennessee, in which all
the operatives are slaves.

But the primary question is, whether the division of
labor which I have proposed, is practicable. Mr. Stanley
says not ; that the manufacturing process " cannot be carried on separately from the other ; for the canes, if not
taken at once to the mill are spoilt." " For this reason,"
he adds, " small farming is out of the question."

Mr. Stanley seems for a moment to have mistaken the side of this question which he was professing to advocate, or else he has proved quite too much for his purpose. If small farms around a central mill cannot be made profitable, because the canes, if not taken at once to the mill are spoilt, then how is it that the present princely estates, into which the island is divided, many of which contain over 3,000 acres a piece, are enabled to crop and manufacture their sugar with only a single mill to each of them?

In the Parish of St. Elizabeth, there are six abandoned sugar estates, averaging each, over three thousand acres. Neither of those estates, when under culture, pretended to have more than one set of sugar works, and yet each one of them, if divided up into twenty-five acre farms, would have endowed one hundred and twenty resident proprietors with a very independent freehold, for a laboring man, within reach of a central mill of ample capacity for the prompt manufacture of all he could produce. The six estates could support seven hundred and twenty earnest, industrious and independent laboring farmers, instead of being abandoned as they have been, for not supporting six unproductive non-resident landlords, and a retinue of equally unproductive book-keepers, agents and attornies.

The same land distributed into five-acre farms would support thirty-six hundred families, who could all carry their canes to one mill and have them ground in due sea-

son. Now, assuming that there are 600,000 acres of good
sugar land in Jamaica, and to every 3,000 acres one central mill was erected, two hundred mills would accommodate 120,000 five-acre tenants just as completely as they
would accommodate 200 three-thousand acre tenants.

But the fact is, one mill properly conducted might
accommodate a much larger area. Elin, the largest sugar
estate in the Parish of St. Elizabeth, embracing 4,650 acres,
uses but one. When we consider that these mills do not
run nights, that steam is not usually got up before nine in
the morning, and the fires as usually go down before five
in the afternoon, it becomes very apparent that they do not
execute more than half the work they might, if properly
pressed and attended. When we farther consider that
proper facilities of internal communication, would enable
planters to deliver their cane at a central mill from twenty-
five to thirty miles distant, on the day it was cut, is any
room left for a doubt that fifty sugar mills of suitable
dimensions and faithfully conducted, would manufacture
the largest sugar crop ever raised in Jamaica, just as well
as eight or ten hundred now do, and probably much
better ?

What is to prevent the planters selling their land, and
with the proceeds enlarging their mills indefinitely ? If
more sugar or coffee can be produced by small proprietors
upon the same surface, it would seem to be the dictate of

ordinary sagacity for the large planters to sell or lease their
lands, build central mills, and become buyers of cane and
manufacturers of sugar and coffee, and such other products of the island as might be turned to best account.

At present, perhaps, the facilities for transportation are not
such as would admit of supplying central mills from a very
great distance, but it is enough for my argument to have
shown, that one set of sugar works will manufacture the
produce of 3,000 acres of sugar land, and not run nights;
and if Mr. Stanley's superior " practical knowledge of West
Indian habits" has led him to the conclusion which he
has adopted, that the culture and the manufacture of sugar
cannot be carried on separately, then I have less reason to
regret my more limited opportunities for observation, than
I had imagined.

The fact is, that if the circulation of capital, and the
alienability of land had been unrestricted, if the non-residence of the landlords and the parliamentary protection
given to their peculiar interests, had not contentrated the
whole reclaimed territory of the island, into the hands of a
few whose interests were not identified with those of the
Jamaicans, central mills would have been in general use
here, long since, and the agriculture of the island would
now have been as independent of its manufacturing, as of
its commercial industry.

That separation is destined to take place soon.   Already,

as I have before stated, the better class of lands are almost
within reach of the masses. As soon as the number of
small proprietors is increased a little, central mills will
rapidly spring into existence, and experience will demonstrate the folly of keeping half the capital of the island,
invested in unnecessary machinery which lies idle four-fifths
of the time.

But Mr. Stanley appeals to experience, and undertakes
to say, that the negro farmers have not raised five pounds
of sugar in any single year for exportation.

While I am not prepared to admit, I have no occasion
to deny the correctness of this statement. The reason why
they have not raised much sugar for exportation, if such be
the fact, is as important as it is obvious; they could employ the little land they acquired to far better advantage.
Even negroes are not generally so stupid as to attempt, on
five or ten acres of land, without capital, to enter into competition with three-fifths of the capital of the island, by
cultivating sugar, where butter is worth thirty-seven and a
half cents a pound, eggs three cents a piece, potatoes six
and a quarter and onions twelve and a half cents a pound,
and other provisions ranging at the same extravagant
prices. They can turn their lands to better account.
They raise supplies for their immediate wants. In that
way they incur none of the expenses of getting their produce to market, for they have a market at home which

never fluctuates, and is always liberal. There is no doubt, I apprehend, that the lands of the negroes produce more in money's worth, than any sugar or coffee estates on the island—in proportion to the surface under cultivation ; and if the number of proprietors were multiplied by the division of estates, as I have suggested, the aggregate product of the cultivated lands would be increased in a like proportion.

CHAPTER XV.

Manufacturing Resources.

WHILE I am fully convinced that by the subdivision of estates, and the division of labor, the aggregate product of sugar, or coffee, or cotton, or anything else, might be greatly increased, I am far from saying that they would be, for I greatly doubt whether other produce might not be made more profitable. Whether they would or would not, depends upon facts, about which I am not fully informed. The state of the market, the character of the soil and climate in different localities, the facilities of transportation, and many other influences, would determine the uses to which the farmer would put his land, and sugar, and coffee, and cotton would only be planted, where they could be grown more profitably than anything else.

My impression is, that capital and labor would be diverted into an infinite variety of new channels, which have hitherto been comparatively unexplored. The island has never manufactured anything but the produce of the sugar cane, and its mechanical resources are entirely undeveloped.

I have mentioned that there is not a saw-mill in Jamaica, and yet there is an extensive market here for sawed lumber of every description, and a finer variety of timber in its forests than can be found anywhere else within an area of equal dimensions. Table provisions too, as I have also stated, are generally higher than in New York, and yet the choicest varieties could be produced here for less than half their cost in the New York market. The rarest kinds of fruits grow wild, and rot under the trees that produce them, which might be delivered in a sound and healthy condition along the whole seaboard of the United States, within six days from the time they were plucked, without a particle of difficulty. There is no good reason why the New York fruit market, in the severest months of winter, should not abound with every tropical fruit in absolute perfection, instead of being limited, as it now is, during the winter season, to flavorless fruits plucked green to prevent decay.*

Then there is an infinite variety of preserves, of oils and essences, that might be manufactured to an indefinite extent from the productions of the country. The fields are overrun with a species of wild pine-apple, from which I

---

* It has been only since the establishment of J. Howard & Son's Chagres line of Steamers, which touch at Jamaica, that this prompt and easy communication with the United States has existed. They average a little less than six days from New York to Jamaica, and although they have not been running quite two years, have already begun to revive our almost extinguished commerce with that island

have seen a finer linen manufactured than ever came from
an Irish loom, while the most valuable drugs and dyewoods
literally infest the island.

To illustrate this supineness a little more in detail : the
cocoa nut, which is one of the most profitable fruits that
the earth produces, is turned to no account whatever by
the Jamaicans, though it grows as luxuriant here as in any
quarter of the globe. I was told, by a gentleman who had
a large number of these trees in full maturity, that he would
esteem them the best property on his estate, if he could
get one dollar a hundred for the nuts, but that there was
a very limited market for them, at any price. And
yet there is no part of this fruit that is not valuable. It
thrives in a sandy soil, and bears, in Jamaica within three
or four years after it is planted. From its flowers the finest
arrack in the world may be distilled, and the best of vine-
gar. A coarse brown sugar may also be prepared from
the flower. The green fruit yields a nutritious and delightful drink, and a more substantial food in the pulp which
contains the liquid. When ripe, the fruit is popular as an
article of diet in all parts of the world. From that fruit a
pure oil may be extracted, which may be manufactured
into candles, soap, and used in a variety of other ways, in
which vegetable oils are available, while the refuse, or oil
cake, as it is called, is a most excellent food for cattle.

A medicinal oil is extracted from the bark, which is

used, I understand, in Ceylon, as an efficacious remedy in cutaneous diseases ; the root is also used for medicinal purposes ; its elastic fibres are sometimes woven into strainers for liquids, while the timber may be used in building, or converted into beautiful articles of furniture. The husk consists of a tough fibre, from which cordage and rigging of the best quality may be manufactured, and the finest stuffing for mattrasses that is used, not excepting hair. I saw some of this fibre manufactured at the Penitentiary in Kingston, for mattrass stuffing. I satisfied myself that if its value were known in America, it would bring a higher price than any commodity now in use for bedding. The specimens that I saw were prepared by the convicts, at a cost, I was told, of six cents a pound. Hair costs in New York, I believe about twenty-five cents.

The process of manufacturing it, is very simple—the husk shells are soaked till perfectly soft, and then pounded out until the fibres are all separated. This was done in the prison by hand-labor, and without the use of machinery, and the article could be produced by them for six cents a pound. By the aid of a very simple machine—something, for instance, like that to which rags in a paper mill are first subjected—it is very apparent, that the cost of manufacturing it might be reduced at least one half. When I asked why machinery was not employed in this department of the prison, I was told that they had not work enough to occupy the convicts if machinery was employed. Of course I had nothing to say to a reason so conclusive.

The supply of these husks would be almost inexhaustible. They have no more use or value here than walnut shells have in the States, and may be had by the ship.load for the mere expense of cartage. A cargo of a thousand tons could be manufactured for a thousand dollars, and be worth in the port of New York not less than $4,000, as soon as the usefulness of the article became generally known.

This is but a glimpse of the inexhaustible manufacturing resources of Jamaica, which only wait the appearance of an interested and industrious class of resident proprietors to be developed. For six or eight months of the year nothing is done on the sugar and coffee plantations. Agriculture, at least as it is conducted at present, does not occupy the laborers more than half their time. During the rainy season, by a skilful application of capital, they might be furnished with full employment in sawing lumber, manufacturing brick, and draining-tiles, tools and implements of husbandry which are now imported altogether, if used ; in putting up drugs and dye stuffs for exportation ; in preparing the cocoa nut and pine-apple fibres for the various uses to which foreign manufacturers might devote them ; in improving the internal communication of the island by the construction of railroads and bridges, and in an infinite variety of ways which it is unnecessary to enumerate. Were the land covered with a population of poor and resident proprietors of small estates, they would soon perceive the advantage of encouraging the investment of capital in these domestic manufactures and arts, as the most direct means of furnishing permanent employment, and, of course, creating a permanent demand for labor.

Nor can I omit to mention here another advantage to result from the multiplication of employments, such as I have been describing, the want of which has weighed heavy upon the prosperity of Jamaica. I refer to the educational influences with which a varied industry surrounds the operative classes. In a country like the United States, where occupations are almost as various as the features of the human countenance, capital is constantly in quest of labor which it educates for its purposes. There is something for the most ignorant and inexperienced operative to do, by which he will acquire skill, and by which his faculties will be developed and quickened. All classes do not grow up under the same set of daily experiences, but in earning their daily bread, each is learning something which improves his understanding and multiplies his resources. The operatives in Jamaica, on the other hand, are all doing the same things substantially. Year after year their whole industrial experience is limited mainly to the culture of sugar and coffee, and the manufactures to which they give rise.

They have no new manufactories to resort to, when they are in want of work, no unaccustomed departments of mechanical or agricultural labor are open to receive them, to stimulate their ingenuity and reward their industry. When they know how to ply the hoe, pick the coffee-berry, and tend the sugar mills, they have learned about all the industry of the island can teach them. If, in the sixteen years during which the negroes have enjoyed their freedom, they have made less progress in civilization than their philanthropic champions have promised or anticipated, let the want I have suggested receive some consideration. It may be, that even a white peasantry would degenerate under such influences. Reverse this, and when the negro has cropped his sugar or his coffee, create a demand for his labor in the mills and manufactories of which nature has invited the establishment on this island, and before another sixteen years would elapse, the world would probably have some new facts to assist them in estimating the natural capabilities of the negro race, of more efficiency in the hands of the philanthropist, than all the appeals which he has ever been able to address to the hearts or the consciences of men.

It is scarcely necessary for me to state, that the tendency of all the influences I have been considering, is to throw

POLITICAL INFLUENCE OF THE AFRICAN.

POLITICAL INFLUENCE OF THE AFRICAN. 157

the land into the possession of those who can and will cultivate it, that is, the colored population, and that its productive capacities will never be known till that has taken place.

There are other than material causes, however, which are conspiring to produce this same result. The political power of the island is rapidly passing into the same hands. The possession of four or five acres of land confers a right to vote on the selection of members of Assembly. The blacks are ambitious to possess and exercise the privilege ; it causes them to be courted and respected. They are daily becoming better acquainted with the advantages which the elective franchise confers, and the prospect of attaining it, is with them one of the strongest incentives to effort and economy. The recent election of several of their order to the Assembly, has greatly inflamed this ambition. It is only a short time since there were no colored people returned to that body. In the last Assembly there were a dozen. No negro ever had a seat there till the session before the last, when one was returned. In the last session there were three. It is safe to say, that in a very few years the blacks and browns will be in a clear majority in the Assembly. They already hold the balance of power.

I have previously stated that the colored members were generally, I do not know but universally, attached to the government, or King's House party ; while the Country party, as the opposition party is called, is composed almost exclusively of white members. The reason of this classification is very obvious, and illustrates the nature of the power possessed by the former. The Country party is composed of the large planters, who pay the most of the taxes, and who need legislative protection. The colored classes in general do not feel the taxes, and have nothing to be protected. The present policy of Downing street, it is well known, is adverse to protection. The planting interest wishes the expenses of the island, and the official salaries reduced ; the appointees of Downing street wish no such thing. The colored people generally care nothing about the expenses of government, for they do not have to pay them, while they are not adverse to high salaries, because the home government sagaciously dispenses a liberal share of the offices and patronage among this part of the population. Probably four-fifths of all the public offices on the island are filled by colored people and negroes.

It is unnecessary to say that this state of things is begetting a serious antagonism between the government and the country parties, and has already gone far to alienate the latter from their allegiance. It discourages and disgusts them. Its more remote tendency is to depreciate the value of every kind of property, but especially of real estate ; and to promote emigration of capitalists and capital from the island. Multitudes of the oldest and most respected white citizens contemplate leaving, and are casting about for new seats.

I scarcely saw a man who had not, more or less deliberately, considered the expediency of abandoning the island. Habitual inertness, domestic ties, straightened resources, ignorance of any means of procuring a support elsewhere, and other causes, discourage most of them from entertaining the purpose long, but in spite of these difficulties, there has been a constant current of emigration of white persons, especially the junior members of families, from the island, for the last two or three years, and the proportion is increasing monthly.

Nor are the vacancies created by emigration and death, supplied by the births in the white families, for there are no schools here for instruction beyond the elementary branches of an English education, and as soon as a child is old enough to receive instruction suitable to the rank and position held usually by the English residents, he has to be sent abroad to obtain it. The most of those who leave, never return to reside, unless under an appointment from the government, for neither business nor professional rewards here, hold out to them any inducements. They can find more lucrative and suitable employment most anywhere else. The consequence is, that the losses from the ranks of the white population, from whatever cause, are not repaired.

Of course the loss of every white man is a loss of capital to a greater or less extent, it strengthens the influences already operating to depress the price of property, increases facilities for the colored people to appropriate it, and is hastening that partition of the soil which I have supposed necessary to a realization of its highest productive power. It is also hastening a result which I have reason to believe the home government anticipate and are prepared for—the gradual occupation of the whole island by the blacks. They see and know that the two races cannot prosper together, if both are free ; that the superior intelligence and advantages of the whites will prevent the blacks from acquiring that independence and self-reliance, which are the sinews of enterprise and the basis of national prosperity ; and as the blacks are so much the more numerous, and enjoy so great an advantage in their natural adaptation to the climate of the tropics, it has been wisely determined to surrender the island to them, as soon as it can be done consistently with the vested rights of the white population.

But the question arises, What shall follow the introduction of a colored Governor into the King's house, a colored Chief Justice upon the Queen's bench, a uniform Assembly of colored representatives, with no white people about, to make them ashamed or afraid ? Will Jamaica then recover ?

She will doubtless progress, but she can never attain the height of her prosperity while she remains a dependance of Great Britain.

Any colonial system of government without representation is essentially vicious; the colonial system of Great Britain is probably worse than any other, for she has not a colony in the world which she has not exhausted, or is not rapidly exhausting.

When the colored people become the proprietors of the property, and have to pay high salaries and oppressive taxes, their relations to the government will be rapidly changed, and they will be thrown into the position now occupied by the Country party. They will clamor for low salaries and probably high duties. They will get neither. What lies beyond, it is scarcely worth while to speculate upon, for before that day Great Britain will inevitably be compelled to modify her colonial policy so radically, at least with respect to her West Indian possessions, as to introduce elements into the question which cannot now be conjectured. Nothing is more probable, in respect to the political fate of the island, twenty years hence, than that it will be one of the United States of America.

It can probably be governed more cheaply and to more profit by our people than by any other, and both nations will probably discover before that period, that their mutual interests may be consulted by the transfer. It is from my

purpose however, now, to consider what would be the consequences of such an event, for before it can happen, in all
probability, a new generation will have taken the place of
the present race of freedmen, whose training and experience will qualify them to take no insignificant part in
shaping the destiny of Jamaica, and of the colored population of the West India islands.

CHAPTER XVI.

Climate—Health.

In Jamaica, almost every variety of climate may be found within a day's journey, except the extreme cold. The island is situated between the parallels of 17° 55' and 18° 31' north latitude, about three degrees farther south than Havana, but it is traversed from east to west, through its whole length, by a range of mountains, varying in height from four thousand to eight thousand feet, and by numerous high ridges intersecting the other range from north to south. These mountains on the island, with the ocean surrounding it, prevent those extremes of heat to which this latitude is exposed. I never found the weather oppressive, though I passed most of my time on the south side and in the vicinity of Kingston, where the thermometer ranges several degrees higher than upon the north side or in the interior.

In the morning, about half-past nine, a brisk breeze sets in from the sea, which lasts during the day, is always pure and soft, and leaves a person who is quiet and not exercising, perfectly comfortable. The sun is very hot, and, of course, its rays must be carefully avoided. A land breeze rises when the sun sets, so strong and cool, that the inhabitants have to keep their windows, having an inland exposure, partly if not entirely closed in their sleeping apartments. Strangers would always find this a wise precaution.

The average heat at Kingston, which is the hottest point upon the island, is 80°. It is about ten degrees hotter, on an average, in the winter than in the summer, and there is a variation of about ten degrees in the thermometer in the course of every twenty-four hours. The following meteorological register was kept at Upper Camp, in the suburbs of Kingston, for Sir J. McGregor, and gives a very authentic and satisfactory view of the climate and meteorology of Jamaica. I found it in Henderson's Jamaica Almanack for 1850.

Months,	Max.	Med	Min.	Wind.	Remarks.
January...	84	78	71	N. & S. E.	Fine, some showers, strong N. winds.
February..	84	73	72	ditto..	Fine and dry, strong sea breezes.
March	86	82	77	ditto..	Ditto, earthquakes felt, ditto ditto.
April......	87	83	79	ditto..	Very dry ditto, moderate ditto.
May	87	81	75	ditto..	Fine. with light showers.
June......	86	82	78	ditto..	Mostly ditto, with heavy ditto.
July.......	89	83	77	ditto..	Many showers, but generally fine.
August....	87	82	77	S. S. W..	Some heavy rain, ditto.
Septemb ..	89	82	76	ditto..	Mornings fine, Noon heavy rains.
October....	86	80	74	ditto..	Some heavy rain, mostly fine.
Novemb...	85	79	73	ditto..	Ditto, ditto.
Decemb....	84	78	73	ditto..	Some rain, generally fine.

Bryan Edwards, writing over fifty years ago, says, " In a maritime situation, where I chiefly resided during the space of fourteen years, the general medium of heat during the hottest months, from July to November (both inclusive), was eighty degrees on Fahrenheit's thermometer. In the other months, viz., from December to May, the thermometer ranges from 70° to 80°. The night air in the months of December and January is sometimes surprisingly cool. I have known the thermometer so low at sunrise as 69° even in the town of Kingston; but in the hottest months, the difference between the temperature of noonday and midnight is not more than 5 or 6°."

There is a very marked difference in temperature between the north and south side of the island, and still more in the beauty and luxuriance of the vegetation.

The soil is less exposed to the protracted droughts which sometimes occur during the winter months on the southern coast. This greater abundance of rain is attended with its disadvantages. The temperature is more variable and the air less genial, and not so well adapted for invalids as that which prevails on the opposite side. The seasons are very different also, on the two sides. On the north, winter ranges from October to March, and a plentiful supply of rain is distributed, in small and occasional showers, throughout the year. On the south side, spring may be said to range from November to April, summer from May to August, and winter from September to October.

The chief alternations of the weather are those which occur in consequence of rains or of their absence. The same periods vary, like the temperature, with the locality. In the mountains, they are earlier, more frequent, and more violent than in the lower country. The spring rains do not usually set in until May, though, occasionally, they come as early as March or April.

I am indebted to Mr. Edward McGeachy, the Crown Surveyor of the island, for much important information about the physical condition of Jamaica, and, among other things, for the following upon the subject of the seasons. The usual accounts of them, he tells me, do not give strangers correct impressions. " No one on the island has been more exposed to heat, and cold and wet, than I have (Mr. McGeachy has resided in Jamaica thirty years), and I am qualified to say, that the trials of the wet seasons are altogether exaggerated. May and October are our usual wet months on the south side, where I reside, during which periods it often rains for a whole week without intermission, then it clears off and the weather is delightful, with occasional mid-day ' plumps ' which last about an hour. The mornings and evenings are almost always dry and safe for driving or walking. On one side of the island the season of vegetation lasts from about May to December, then it becomes dry. But not so, on the north side, which is usually quite wet during the winter months. Various parts of the island are wetter or dryer, according to the structure of the country and the degree of its cultivation, a knowledge of which, will enable persons to command at all seasons most delightful residences."

It is one of the advantages of a residence near Kingston that at any time in half a day's drive, one can command cool weather. I left that city one morning on horseback about half-past eight, and drove to Cold Spring Gap, in the mountains, about 4,200 feet above the level of the sea, in five hours, where I found the weather chilly, and was soon glad to descend to a warmer temperature. A little lower down, the climate is delightful. But nothing can be imagined more picturesque than this ride from Kingston to Cold Spring. We passed through the Hope Estate, which was part of the immense fortune of the Duke of Buckingham, whose bankruptcy rang through all the public journals a year or two ago. After riding some distance on a road which was bounded on every side by the most luxuriant tropical vegetation, we came to the Middleton Coffee Estate, which also belonged to the Buckingham property. The coffee culture marks a lower temperature. All these estates lie along the sides of the mountains. We also drove through what is called the "Cold Spring Coffee Field," which is owned in London by a Mr. Hamilton, and is said to produce the finest coffee that is taken into Liverpool, where it commands 140s. per cwt. The estate embraces about one hundred acres.

A little farther up we reached New Castle, which is about 4,000 feet above the level of the sea, and has been selected by the government as a military station, on account of its coolness and salubrity; about 600 men are quartered here. Another hour's drive brought us to Cold Spring Gap, about five hundred feet higher. Here we were surrounded by a dense fog, which prevented our enjoying the scenery, and before we got off, we were overtaken by a shower, the common experience of those who make this expedition.

The change of temperature and scenery, and vegetation, which one encounters in passing from Kingston to Cold Spring, is so great, that it is difficult for the visitor to realize that he is within the tropics. Above New Castle, we no longer see the orange or the star apple, but the American apple, the peach, the strawberry, and other summer fruits of the temperate zones, flourish in perfection. At and for some distance below New Castle, the nights are very cool, and blankets are indispensable at night, and fires not unfrequently. Neither are ever required in Kingston. At Cold Spring the thermometer ranges from 55° to 65°, and it has been observed as low as 44°. There a fire at noon-day is comfortable a great part of the year.

The most delightful climate that can be imagined, is to be found back of Kingston, upon an elevation of about

2,000 feet, where every tropical fruit thrives, and where the nights are always cool, and the heat of the day is never oppressive. It would be difficult to select a residence in any part of the globe more healthful and more luxuriantly endowed by nature.

Jamaica is generally a healthy island. It cannot be said to be subject to any malignant fevers. The yellow fever which used to prevail, does not visit the island as often as it visits New York, and is not more fatal when it does come.

Dr. King, pastor of Grey Friars' Church, Glasgow, visited Jamaica about a year ago for the health of a member of his family, who was consumptive. Since his return, he has printed a small volume of his observations, in which I find the following on the subject I am now considering, and to which he was likely to have given special attention:

"So far as I could form an opinion from what I witnessed myself, and learned from my intercourse with physicians, the estimate generally entertained of the unhealthiness of Jamaica greatly exceeds the truth. Many diseases very fatal in Britain are unknown there, or they are found only in modified and gentle forms. So it is with hooping-cough and measles. The complaint most common in the island is fever. In most cases it is slight and transient, and occasions little suffering or alarm. It is liable, however, to become virulent, especially if persons are so imprudent as to get wet and not change their clothing, or if they make fatiguing journeys in the heat of the day, or pass the night in the neighborhood of lagoons and marshes. As respects yellow fever, about which so much is said here, it there rages as an epidemic at times, but it is far from being a prevalent disease in the island. Its characteristic is the 'black vomit,' and I met with different physicians who, after practising for many years, had never seen fever accompanied with this symptom. There were some such cases at Montego Bay when I arrived there, but they were few, and I heard of no more of them so long as I was in the colony.

Many of the physicians in the island administer calomel and quinine, in very large doses, to all persons affected with fever. But others of them condemn this mercurial treatment as carried destructively far; and they ascribe to it much of that debility of constitution with which a proportion of the colonists are afflicted, and which is commonly charged on the enervating tendency of the climate.

I could not learn of an instance where an invalid, or any of his friends coming to Jamaica to spend a single winter had died of fever. Persons affected with pulmonary complaints are considered particularly secure from its attacks."

Elsewhere, in speaking of the class of invalids most likely be benefitted by a visit to Jamaica, he says:

" A physician of eminence in the island said to me, that where hectic fever was strong and constant, the patient should not come to Jamaica, as its warmth would probably increase the fever, and thus prove prejudicial; but if the pulse did not indicate much fever, he thought that the patient, even although reduced and enfeebled, had great inducement to make trial of the colony, as he never found any, in these circumstances, fail of being benefitted by making it a temporary place of residence."

There are some precautions however, which need to be carefully observed by persons from a northern climate visiting Jamaica. They should be careful not to lay off flannel if accustomed to wear it, and to put it on, if they are not accustomed to it. A thin flannel next the skin is uniformly worn by the white inhabitants, and is indispensible to a stranger. It is unwise to dress too thinly over flannel. I found many old residents in Kingston wearing black cloth coats and pantaloons, and hats all the time, and some of them told me they never wore any other than cloth outer garments. I tried it myself during the last week of my stay upon the island, and was not conscious of feeling the heat any more oppressive than when I wore linen altogether. The strong and steady breezes by day and night, make woollen garments a necessary protection from the sudden changes of temperature to which the surface of the skin is constantly exposed here.

To my own countrymen, it may be well enough to say, that in preparing to visit this island, it is not worth their while to supply themselves largely with under clothing, as woollens of all kinds and linens can be procured here much cheaper than in the United States.

Strangers should be cautious about sleeping with their windows open towards the land. The night air is chilly and damp, and sometimes impregnated with malaria from distant marshes and lagoons. It is not however, in my judgment, as dangerous as the night air on the banks of the Hudson.

The temptation to indulge in fruit to excess here, is so great as to make a word of caution upon that point not superfluous. It is generally supposed that one cannot eat too many oranges, for example, and as they abound here in perfection, the error becomes as serious as it is common. It is never worth while to eat more than two or three oranges in the course of a day, and though more may sometimes be eaten with impunity, a more free indulgence is very apt to induce a feverish and morbid condition of the system. Of other fruits, the same temperance needs to be observed. All that is required is the exercise of a little judgment, not forgetting, amid these unaccustomed bounties of nature, the proportions of fruit and vegetable diet to which your constitution is accustomed.

Keep out of the sun as much as practicable, and avoid of all things, violent and heating exercises until you understand the symptoms by which your constitution reveals the influence of the climate upon it. A stranger

who is not accustomed to a warm climate, may induce a
dangerous fever by a single excess of this kind. Wet
clothes are equally to be avoided ; if only dampened by
the dew, they should be promptly changed.

Musquitoes abound in Jamaica, and as soon as the sun
sets, become a serious annoyance. The traveller will do
well to provide himself in advance, with a good musquito
net of a fine texture, with which he can protect himself
from them entirely. Those to be procured in Jamaica,
are generally too dense, and affect the circulation of the
air.

There are so few facilities for travelling upon the island,
that the stranger who wishes to go about much, will do
well to buy a horse and wagon immediately upon his
arrival, at a cost of a couple of hundred dollars. With
these he can travel when and where he pleases, and if he
buys judiciously, can sell them when he wishes to, for
nearly what they cost. The expense of journeying in this
way will be greatly reduced, and the comfort proportionately increased.

The boarding houses are all kept by colored people.
The price of board ranges from one to two dollars a day,
in the better class of houses. According to the English
custom, the boarder pays only for his room and for such
meals as he orders. Nothing is done here punctually,
and it is useless to attempt to have meals served at regular

and uniform hours.   I found nothing punctual in Jamaica
but the railroad and the sea and land breezes.

The following letter, received recently from a gentleman residing in Kingston, whom I have had occasion to
quote once or twice before in the course of these pages,
contains some further information upon many of the points
to which I have referred, of sufficient interest to justify
me in inviting to it the attention of my readers.   It will
be found a useful commentary upon some of the preceding chapters, which were all written and printed before
its receipt.

KINGSTON, JAMAICA,
23d Sept., 1850.

MY DEAR SIR :
    *   *   *   *   I feel assured that this "Italy of the
West," and its proximity to your country, need only to be
known to induce your men of enterprize to spend a portion
of their time with us.   You know we have perpetual summer, and that there is a springing vegetation in every
month of the year.   The products of our soil are very
varied.   I think wheat, if cultivated, would succeed.   But
I would refer rather to what is certain, such as Indian corn,
millet, peas of all kinds, sugar, coffee, cocoa, ginger,
pimento, indigo, cotton, flax plants, yams, cassedy, arrow
root, tobacco, a variety of oil-producing nuts, grapes, figs,
and all tropical fruits in abundance, for which now there is
easy access to the American market.   These things, at
least some of them, command a high price on the spot,

particularly Indian corn; wheat usually sells at from 75
cents to $1,25 per bushel. For grapes it is not unusual
to pay 50 cents per pound. I paid not very long ago,
$4,50 for a barrel of potatoes. These prices will surprise
you when I aver, that two hours a day of work with the
hoe, will suffice to enable a man to obtain abundance of
food for the year. The food of the island which is not
imported, is raised, not by farmers using implements of
husbandry, but almost entirely by the middle class of
negro laborers in the country, who often carry a basket full
on their heads, 15 or 20 miles to a market. One of your
small farmers would economize his labor, and bring similar
products to market in a cart, cheaper, with a profit of 75
per cent.

I wish we had a large, a very large importation of your
colored people who have been accustomed to farming.
Our climate, and whole state of society, would suit them
infinitely better than Liberia, and it would be a cheaper
course for them to a comfortable home.

Great bargains of land, with buildings on it, may still
be had here. The sum expended on the purchase of what
is called an "improved farm" in the western states, would
purchase here in many cases, a large tract of land with
buildings. Visitors of every taste, and for every variety of
object, may probably visit us, now that the way is rendered
so easy and pleasant by the steamers. The most beautiful
secluded retirements in a delightful Italian climate in the
mountains, may be purchased for a trifling amount, say
from 2 to 3,000 dollars; but large tracts of fine land may
be purchased in many districts for 1 or 2 dollars an acre,

and a comfortable living may be made out of it by a very small amount of labor. When I consider the hardships of settlers in your new states, with the cold, frost, snow and damp they must encounter, and ice-bound during many months of the year, I wonder very much that all who are not of the most robust frames of body, do not prefer our levels to settle on.

There is an old prejudice against our climate. It arose *not* amongst the first settlers, who praised it for its delightsome salubrity, but amongst those who followed them, a reckless, dissipated, over-wrought race, who cherished habits which the least reflection would have forbidden, and which in these days have almost wholly disappeared. There is a great deal of immorality always incident to slave countries. We are here, doubtless, subject to disease : to fevers particularly, but of the most manageable kind, generally. Your fevers are much worse, and your liability to colds and inflammatory attacks very much more I believe, endanger life than our fevers would. To the timid visitors, I would safely say, that there is no risk to life in spending a winter here, so great as the risk attendant on a winter residence in America. I think there is much less, and in numerous, very numerous instances, life is saved and greatly prolonged to a large class of individuals by residence here.

To invalids it will be a recommendation that we have abundance of medical men, of the highest qualifications that British training can confer : men of true science, great experience, and unfailing assiduity. You cannot in New York command higher skill I hardly believe. I am unwilling to extend this letter, already too long, except to say that what I have written, I have carefully considered, feeling the responsibility of a recommendation which if not well founded, might expose me to reproach. I feel strong partiality to the country after a residence in it of upwards of 17 years, and so much do I like the climate, that I feel the greatest repugnance to change it, unless for the important consideration of education to my boys, whom I intend to remove from England to America, that they may be nearer to me, and pay me or I pay them, a visit during the holidays, once or twice a year. I feel that by our easy access to your country, the value of property, and the advantages generally of a residence here, are very greatly increased. Believe me to be,

My dear sir,

Very truly yours,

WM. WEMYSS ANDERSON.

JOHN BIGELOW, Esq.

CHAPTER XVII.

CONCLUSION.

ALIENATION OF LAND.

THERE are some difficulties attending the alienation of land, in Jamaica, which tend to prevent its sale to small capitalists. In the first place, many of the owners reside abroad and have to be consulted before their island agents can negotiate. In the next place, the estates are very liable to be involved in an entail in some way, so that the fee cannot be transferred. Then the titles sometimes run back through a long series of years, and their examination involves considerable expense oftentimes, and as English conveyancers have to be employed and paid English measure, the tax for conveying property, is something of a discouragement to the purchase of small freehold properties. When the title of a large estate is in a resident who wishes to sell the whole or parts of it, the matter is very much simplified, for he can have the title to himself, properly authenticated, and then all who purchase under him take no risks against which it is not very easy to be insured.

Foreigners, however, should bear in mind that no title to real property can vest in them, under any circumstances, without they have taken out letters of naturalization, under the great seal of the Governor of the island. To obtain these " letters," an oath of allegiance to the government of Great Britain must be taken. As many of my countrymen have manifested some inclination to purchase winter residences in Jamaica, they may feel an interest in seeing the laws which define the terms upon which aliens may hold a title to real estate here. They are as follows:

" 35 Car. 2d, c. 3.—It shall be lawful for the Governor, by instrument under the broad seal of this island, to make any alien or foreigner, who shall come to settle and plant in this island, having first taken the oath of allegiance, to be to all intents and purposes fully naturalized, and every such person so, approved and named in such letters patent, shall, by virtue of this act, have and enjoy, to himself and his heirs, such immunities and rights of and unto laws and privileges of this island, in as full and ample manner as any natural born subjects of the Crown have or enjoy within the same, as if he had been born within any of the realms or dominions of England."

" 13 Geo. 3d, c. 14.—It shall be lawful for any person, being a foreigner, or an alien, to lend money at lawful interest, upon the security of any freehold or leasehold estates in this island, and to hold the same as an effectual security for the money lent."

" Ib. sec. 2.—On forfeiture of any such security made to such foreigner or alien, and the non-payment of the money so lent or due thereon, at the time therein stipulated, the legal estate upon which such mortgage shall have been granted, shall from thenceforth become vested in the pre- sident of the council, the speaker of assembly and the chief justice of this island, for the time being, upon such trusts, and for such uses, intents and purposes as shall be expressed in the original conveyances or securities made to the foreigner, or alien, for the money lent, and it shall be lawful for every such foreigner or alien, his heirs, execu- tors, administrators or assigns, to bring and prosecute by him or his lawful attorney, his action or bill, in any court of law or equity in this island, in the names of the trus- tees before mentioned, for the recovery of the money lent and due upon such securities, by sale or otherwise, as effectually as natural subjects may do; and such trustees are hereby required to allow their names to be used in bringing or prosecuting such actions or bills for the pur- poses aforesaid. Provided always, that no such foreigner or alien, shall, by any means whatever, be entitled to ob- tain, or enter into the actual possession of any such lands or estates, or to foreclose the equity of redemption thereof."

It will be perceived that an alien may take a mortgage, but upon a forfeiture and sale, the property cannot come to him. The proceeds, as far as they go to the satisfaction of his claim, will be paid to him, but the property remains in the custody of ex-officio trustees, indicated by the statute.

A professional friend, residing in Jamaica, whom I consulted about the best mode for aliens to get an interest in real property here, sent me the following suggestions in a note containing the above extracts from the statute. They may be relied upon, as far as they go.

" It appears to me that Americans desirous of obtaining an interest in land here, ought to hold it in the name of a British subject, resident in America, in whom they have full confidence, who might, if required, give them the farther security of a mortgage for a sum equal to the price, taken on such terms as to render the sale as easy and direct as possible. It would not be necessary to register the mortgage, unless by the death of the holder of the land without an heir or devisee capable of executing a conveyance, it should become necessary to realize the value of the property by a sale under the mortgage. To obviate any perplexity from the death of the holder of the land, it might be desirable to have two holders, so that in case of the death of one, the title might survive to the other.

It is a pity that any such indirect course should be requisite, and I believe that similar difficulties as to such holdings exist in all countries. It is considered a necessary policy.

A respectable alien might, I think, be at all times safe from molestation to his title under the justice and generosity of our public officers. The moral sense of the community would be outraged, beyond endurance, were any attempt made to invoke the letter of the law to deprive an alien of what was honestly his. Think for a moment of the reprisals it would provoke against British subjects holding land in America, as many do with all safety, contrary to the letter of your laws. Your worthy citizens, would, I am sure, consider it infamous, as we would, to disturb such a holder.

Such a management, however, of the title, as I have suggested may be preferred by cautious people.

I mentioned British subjects *resident in America*, as the proper intermediate holders of such property, but your countrymen who come, desirous of settling amongst us for temporary purposes, would in very few cases be at a loss to find safe holders of their interests in land amongst the friends they would make here."

Were aliens permitted to hold property here, it is probable that the United States would very soon furnish white laborers in sufficient quantities to show the agricultural capabilities of the island; but there are very few, if any Americans worth having as fellow citizens, who would renounce their native country and take the oath of allegiance to any foreign sovereign. I have no doubt, however, in my own mind, that the title of an American purchaser in good faith, and his heirs, executors and assigns, would be as fully protected in Jamaica as in the United States, during the continuance of peace between the two countries. If a war should occur, it would be unsafe to reckon upon a continuance of such protection.

The alienation and management of property incurs the following government expenses:

Every mortgage for £200, pays a stamp duty of £1; a mortgage for £1,000, pays £4; for £3,500, pays £10; and for £5,000, pays £15.

A lease, where the yearly rent is less than £100, pays a stamp duty of 10s; when over £200 and under £300, it pays £1; where it exceeds £1,000, it pays £3.

Leases of waste and uncultivated lands, to the poor or laboring classes, for terms not beyond three lives, or ninety-nine years, are exempt from these duties.

Powers of attorney pay the following stamp duties:

To recover debts, or for the sale of property, £1

To manage a pen, plantation or sugar estate, £3.

If only a place of residence, moorland, or both, £1 6s.

Any other kind of power, £1.

OCEAN STEAMERS.

THE facilities of communication and correspondence between Jamaica and New York, have been greatly increased within the past two years. There are now four first class steamers, of from 1,200 to 2,000 tons, running from New York to Chagres, all of which stop, both going out and returning, at Kingston. The line that was first established, owed its existence to the enterprise of J. Howard & Son, shipping merchants, of New York city, who directed the Crescent City, then running to Chagres, to adopt Kingston as a coaling depot. She made her first visit to the island in the month of December, 1848. Shortly after, the more splendid steamer Empire City, of 2,000 tons, was completed and put upon the line, since when there has been an uninterrupted semi-monthly communication. Almost immediately after this line was established, our government contracted with the proprietors, for the carriage of the mails between the two ports; since when, the intercourse between the United States and the British West India islands has been growing daily more intimate.

Two more first-class steamers have been placed on this route, by Messrs. Howland & Aspinwall, of New York, within the past year, making four in all, by which a sure, safe, and punctual conveyance between the two countries is always at command. The fare in these steamers, either way, for first cabin, $100 ; for second cabin, $80 ; and for steerage, $50.

The voyages average about six days. No instance has yet occurred, I believe, of any steamer being over seven days in going either way.

POST-OFFICE DEPARTMENT.

There is a general post office in Kingston, and there are forty-two other provincial offices. There is but one daily mail, and that is crrried between Kingston and Spanishtown. Mails are despatched from Kingston every Monday and Thursday afternoons, at half-past five o'clock, to all parts of the island. The return mail arrives on Wednesdays and Saturdays, and delivered at nine A. M., making two country mails per week. A letter not exceeding half an ounce, to be conveyed not exceeding 60 miles, is charged 8 cents, over 60 miles and under 100, 12 cents, over 100 and under 200, 16 cents.

NEWSPAPERS.

There are two daily newspapers published in Jamaica, both at Kingston. The oldest is the *Kingston Journal*, established in 1838, and edited by Robert Jordan and Robert Osborne, both colored men. This is the organ of the government, and its proprietors are printers for the Assembly. They are both also members of that body.

The *Colonial Standard* is the name of the other daily. It was established in 1849, by W. Girod, a talented and energetic Englishman, who was formerly the editor of another once popular journal, the Kingston Dispatch, which he left in consequence of a difference of opinion with his associate, and which has become extinct. The *Standard* is the organ of the country party, and devoted to the advocacy of a protective tariff, reduction of salaries and the importation of labor from Africa. Mr. Girod is a good scholar and a vigorous writer, but rather an incau-

tious politician.   He also occupies a seat in the Assembly.
There are three semi-weekly journals printed in Jamaica,
the *Cornwall Chronicle*, at Montego Bay, established in
1781, of which Alexander Holmes is editor ; the *Cornwall
Courier*, at Falmouth, established in 1832, and edited by
Edward Burns : and the *Falmouth Post*, at the same
place, established in 1835, and edited by John Costello.

The highest circulation of the dailies, is from 600 to 800.
That of the provincials is more limited.

All these papers are under the editorial management of
cultivated men, and the original articles very uniformly,
betray a degree of taste and scholarship which is rarely to
be found in American journalism.   But their columns are
chiefly filled with extracts from English journals, and accounts of what is doing " at home," by which the stranger
may perceive at once, that Jamaica has a transitory and
dependent population, and that she inspires among them
no feeling of nationality or sentiment of home.

APPENDIX A.

A Visit to the Emperor of Haiti.

"On my arrival at Port-au-Prince, my first care was to ask M. Raybaud (the French consul,) to present me to the man who at the present moment, is the centre of attraction, admiration and envy in this remote portion of the globe. After a delay of a few days, M. Raybaud informed me that the desired interview would be granted, and that it had been arranged that it should take place on the following day. At the appointed time we went to the Palace. This edifice, which was in former times the residence of the governors of St. Domingo, assumes an imposing and even royal appearance when compared with the wretched hovels of which the rest of the town is composed. In point of fact, however, it would be considered very mediocre in any country where architecture has made some progress. The palace is very low, being composed of only one story, raised a few feet from the ground, and approached by four or five steps, which extend all around the edifice. A court which is railed in, and in which the Emperor passes a review of his troops every Sunday, reminds one vaguely of that of the Tuilleries. On entering the palace we were shown into a waiting room, which I examined

with attention.   The floor is in white marble, the furniture
in black hair-cloth and straw.   On a richly carved table
appeared a beautiful bronze clock, representing the arms
of Haiti—namely, a palm-tree surrounded with fascines of
pikes and surmounted with the Phrygian cap.   The walls
were decorated with two fine portraits, hung so as to cor-
respond with each other.   The one represents the celebrated French conventionist, the Abbe Gregoire, and the
other the reigning Emperor of Haiti.   The former is the
work of an European artist ; the latter does honor to the
talent of a mulatto artist, the Baron Colbert.   I should,
perhaps, have remarked more, if my attention had not
been attracted by the step of his Majesty in the neighboring apartment, into which we were presently ushered.
This apartment is hung with the portraits of all the great
men of Haiti, and it is in it that the grand receptions are
given.   We immediately approached his Majesty, who was
dressed in a handsome green uniform, irreproachable either
in material or form.   He wore two gold epaulettes orna-
mented with two silver stars ; a *plaque*, provisionally orna-
mented with crystal, decorated his breast.   He had a sword
by his side, and carried his hat in his hand.   He commenced by giving us a very cordial shake of the hand.
He then sat down on a *fauteuil*, and waited with appearance of confusion and timidity, till M. Raybaud addressed
him.   We had, at his invitation, sat down upon chairs.   The
consul, after mentioning my name and profession, informed the Emperor that I had come to visit his empire simply
from motives of curiosity and amusement, and that it
would have been a great disappointment to me if I had

been obliged to leave the island without having had the honor of being received by his Majesty. To this speech, I added, 'Sire, it was the only object of my voyage,' at the same time half rising from my seat. The Emperor imitated my movement, and thanked me, adding at the same time, 'I have already had the pleasure of seeing this gentleman at the review on Sunday.' It was now my turn to offer my thanks for this flattering reminiscence. The conversation continued in the same manner for about twenty minutes. When we rose to take our leave of the Emperor, he again shook hands with us. Three salutations on our part, and as many on his, concluded the ceremony.

"Faustin Soulouque is completely black, but his features have not by any means, that savage and hideous form which ignorance attributes to the negroes of purely African origin. On the contrary, his features are pleasing, and there is a peculiar sweetness in his smile. Though 64 years of age, he does not appear to be more than 50. In height he is middle-sized. His breast is large and projecting, his shoulders broad, and his haunches clumsy, like those for which Louis XVIII was peculiar. From the regularity of his features, his profile looks like that of a Roman Emperor. When standing, his corpulence makes him appear little. Though naturally taciturn, he is always dignified and choice in his words. It is right to rectify an error which attributes to him an entire ignorance of the French language. In my presence he spoke very correctly, and without any mixture of creolicisms. He has also been accused of not being able either to read or right. The truth is, that he signs his name legibly, and even in cases of necessity writes letters, and besides that, he reads every evening, without the aid of a secretary, the new history of Haiti, which has just been published by M. Modion, a native of much merit, and has recently been created a baron. He is greatly annoyed at the caricatures of him published in the Paris *Charivari*, and the jokes of the press in general. On this point he is susceptible to an incredible extent.

"Faustin Soulouque is of the most humble origin. He was born a slave on the property of M. Viallet. This gentleman, who is an European, has been pointed out to me. He has succeeded in escaping all the revolutionary storms which have agitated this country, and at present is an inhabitant of Port-au-Prince. The Emperor Soulouque having one day recently met him, went up to him and said, 'Although I am an Emperor to the rest of the world, I cannot but look upon you as my master.' 'And I,' replied M. Viallet, 'consider myself as your subject.' How strange are human destinies!

"At the period of the evacuation of Haiti by the French, the emancipated slave entered as a soldier the army of General Dessalines. From step to step, he rose to the rank of colonel, and he held that rank at the period of the fall of the President Boyer, a grave event, in which the present Emperor was not at all implicated. From this taciturnity— a quality which among the blacks is considered to denote the most approved wisdom and discretion—he was admitted into the secret of the several conspiracies which succeeded each other from 1843 to 1847. Having been created a general of division under Richer, he only owed his election as Emperor to the accident of his name having been mentioned in the Senate at the moment when the votes were divided between two candidates, neither of whom had a sufficient majority. He then became the means of conciliation between the parties. The blacks voted for him on account of his ebony skin, the mulattos because they thought they had no reason to fear the ambition of one who had till then been quite unknown. But the latter were not long in discovering that they had given to themselves a master, and not a flexible instrument. Hence proceeded the sanguinary events of the month of April, 1848.

"Soulouque triumphed in consequence of his displaying a terrible energy of character. His victory was disgraced by some frightful executions. Perfidious counsellors drove him into a course of vengeance, speaking of nothing less than exterminating the whole colored race, who form the fifth of the population of Haiti. In this state of matters, the consul-general of France acquired for ever the gratitude of humanity. In the midst of the balls which whistled through the streets of Port-au-Prince, he repaired to the chief of the state, and succeeded, after reiterated efforts, in obtaining from him an amnesty, which excluded only twelve persons whose safety had been already secured. In departing with the good news M. Raybaud said to Soulouque, 'President, of all the persons here present, I am the only one who does not depend on you, and my opinion should appear to you at least the most disinterested. Many of these persons (pointing to the instigators of the crime,) excite your resentment as much as possible, and drive you to the most sanguinary measures, without in the least troubling themselves about the opinion that will be entertained of you beyond this island.' These last words made the greatest impression on the mind of Soulouque, and the hand of the conqueror, ready to strike the conquered, was arrested by this appeal to the tribunal of civilized nations. Soulouque for the last two years was principally occupied in re-conquering the Spanish part of the island, erected into the Dominican Republic, when, to the surprise of the European press, he was proclaimed Emperor. People have generally agreed in saying that he did not solicit this advancement; and, at any rate, he did not yoke himself a plagiarist of an idea which has always been attributed to another President.

" The name of Emperor expresses nothing Napoleon-like at Haiti; it supposes only an authority better respected than that of President, and recalls to the Haitians the popular recollection of Dessalines, who, in reward to the services rendered to his country, had been proclaimed Emperor. The following is, in few terms, the way in which the change in the form of government was brought about:—A certain number of military and civil citizens addressed, on the 20th of August, 1849, a petition to the Chamber of Representatives, demanding that the title of Emperor should be conferred on his excellency the President Soulouque. General Vil Luban, commandant of the garrison of Port-au-Prince, expressed the same wish, as well as the principal officers present in the capital. On the 25th, the Chamber took cognizance of the petition, approved it, and transmitted it on the same day to the Senate, who gave it their sanction. Not a voice was raised in defence of the expiring republic. On the 26th, the two great powers of the State conveyed his promotion to Soulouque, accompanied with a crown and a cross, and expressed their devotion in the most monarchical terms. The *coup d'etat*, if such it be, was accompanied with the legal forms, and met with no opposition anywhere. The constitution was immediately put into harmony with the new order of things. Such as it is at present, it guarantees the essential rights of citizens, and leaves, in appearance, little latitude of arbitrary proceedings. Unfortunately, here, as elsewhere, practice continually contradicts theory. Entering completely into his imperial *role*, Faustin I. did not delay creating orders and titles of nobility. He is greatly honored for his conception, so favorably received by the Haitians, who, amongst other resemblances to their former rulers, have always been as vain as cocks. There are at present two orders in the empire—the military order of St. Faustin, and the civil order of the Legion of Honor. The Emperor proclaimed himself the grand master, and has made grand crosses, and commanders and knights. The titles are those of princes, dukes, counts, barons and knights. The princes and the dukes have been chosen amongst the generals of division and the vice admirals; the counts amongst the generals of brigade and the rear-admirals; the barons amongst the adjutant generals, the colonels and captains in the navy; the knights amongst the lieutenant colonels and commanders of the navy. An assimilation of grades has been in some measure established between the civil and the military functionaries.

The senators, the representatives, the judges, the superior officers of the customs, &c., are all barons. For the wo-men, besides the feminine of the titles accorded to the men, there exists the special title of Marchioness. The first ordinance decrees the creation of four princes and fifty-seven dukes. The princes, named at the same time Marshals of the Empire, were the Generals Pierrot, La-zarre, Souffraud and Bobo. They receive, with the title of Most Serene Highness, that of Lord. To the ducal quality is attached the title of His Grace, and the name of some locality. From this after circumstance arise the denomi-nations which have led astray the European and American journals. Thus Gen. Geffrard is Duke of the Table, Gen. Luiding, is Duke of Marmalade, Gen. Segrattier, Duke of Frose-Bonbon, Gen. Alberti, Duke of Lemonade, &c. But the Table, Marmalade, Frose-Bonbon, Lemonade, &c., are all places marked in the ancient geography of the country. King Christopher already made use of them for the same purpose as Soulouque, and wittily said, ' The French, when they laugh at my Marmalade and Lemonade, forget that they have amongst themselves *des Pois* and *des Bouillon*.' These two illustrious names are certainly lost in the dark-ness of times ; but have we not seen in our own day M. Salvandy desirous of being called Count de Chante-Merle ? The princes and dukes are all grand crosses of the order of St. Faustin, and all have the grand cordon of the Le-gion of Honor. Another ordinance produced at once ninety-one counts. They are all styled Excellency, and their titles, like those of the dukes, are taken from different localities. Thus we have, amongst others, the Count de la

Serinque, the Count de Guepes, the Count de Diamant,
the Count de Perches, the Count de la Bombarde, &c.
All the counts are commanders of the order of St. Faustin
and officers of the Legion of Honor. More prodigal of
his favors as he descends in the scale of aristocracy, the
Emperor has created an innumerable mass of barons and
knights. Louis XIV, in the midst of his splendors, did
not perhaps imagine as many honorary changes as the
Emperor Faustin. Amongst his household, figure a grand
almoner, a grand master of the pantry, a grand marshal
of the palace, a quarter master, gentlemen of honor, governors of the royal palaces and castles, pages, masters of
ceremonies, librarian, heralds at arms, &c. The Empress
Adelina has likewise her household, which is composed
of a grand almoner, two ladies of honor, two tire-women,
fifty-six ladies of the palace, twenty-two ladies of the cha-
pel, (all duchesses, countesses, baronesses, ladies of knights,
or marchionesses,) chamberlains, grooms, pages, &c. The
imperial princess, Madame Olivia Faustin, possesses an
equally brilliant household. Her gouvernante is Madame
le Chevalier de Bonheur. The costume of the nobility
has been regulated with particular care. The princes,
dukes and counts must wear white tunics, the barons red
coats, and the knights blue coats. They are, moreover,
distinguished by the number of plumes in their hats. The
princes have nine, the dukes seven, the counts five, the
barons three and the knights two. An ordinance decress
in minute terms the etiquette of the court. The gentlemen
must appear in uniform; the ladies in full dress. 'The
nobles guard their swords,' the ordonnance says, ' as their

finest ornament.' The *tabouret* is reserved for the princes
and princesses, the dukes and duchesses, whilst folding
chairs are allowed to counts and countesses, barons and baronesses, knights and their ladies.   Soulouque is actively
occupied in raising Haiti to the height of the ancient mo-
narchies of Europe.   Ideas of war engage him without
intermission—a brave soldier, he is determined to efface
the defeat of Azud, where a few hundred Dominicans, pro-
fiting by the inaction of the Haitian army, gained an easy
victory.   Two war steamers have been ordered in Europe.
The campaign is to open next month.   The chances appear very bad for St. Domingo, the population of which is
only about 150,000, whilst that of Haiti is upward of
600,000.   The unfortunate republic has already in vain
appealed to the protection of France and England, and
now solicits the intervention of a power of the second order.
Reduced to extremities, she may cast herself into the arms
of the United States ; such an eventuality might occasion
grave complications.   What especially encourages Soulouque in his warlike projects is, that the excellent sale of
coffee, the principal article of export, increases greatly the
resources of this year.   The system of monopoly introduced by the minister of finance, M. Solomon, has been
crowned with complete success, however contrary it may
appear to sound notions of political economy.   The ordinary revenue of Haiti is valued at about £240,000 ; official situations are paid accordingly.   The Emperor receives about £3,200 a year, the Empress from £1,000 to
£1,200, the three ministers have each a little less than
£120 a year as their salary.   The French indemnity

weighs heavily on the budget. The clergy costs very little; there are not more than forty-eight priests in the whole bounds of the empire. People have been mistaken when they spoke of the influence of the Jesuits at the court of Port-au-Prince. The Haitian territory is closed against all monastic orders. The Vicar Apostolic, the Abbe Cessens, who has been represented as the agent of the disciples of Loyola, strictly confines himself to the religious duties of his charge. As for the authority of the ministers, it is to be wished that it were somewhat greater. They are men of acknowledged merit. M. Duiresue, minister of foreign affairs, of the interior, of war and of marine, would shine in the most civilized countries. He is a clear mulatto. M. Solomon, minister of finance and of commerce, and M. Francisque, minister of justice and of worship, are jet black. In conclusion, and to resume my general impressions of Haiti, I must say, that I found the elements of civilization in a country which has been supposed to be completely plunged in barbarism. In all social relations, I have only had to congratulate myself on the character of the inhabitants. The highways afforded a security which appears fabulous. In the towns, I met all the charms of civilized life. The graces of the ladies of Port-au-Prince will never be effaced from my recollection."

APPENDIX B.

A Tabular Return of Exports from the Island of Jamaica for sixty-one years, ending the 10th of Oct. 1848.

Year when exported.	Sugar. Hhds.	Rum. Punch's	Molasses. Casks.	Ginger. Pounds.	Pimento. Pounds.	Coffee. Pounds.	Remarks.
1772	76,109					840,558	
1773	80,738					779,303	
1774	75,781					739,039	
1775	81,404					439,981	
1788	89,340					1,035,368	
1789	91,021					1,492,282	
1790	91,181					1,783,740	
1791	91,020					2,299,874	August—Destruction of St. Domingo.
1793	82,138	35,194	—	1,063,600	1,968,560	3,938,576	
1794	97,124	40,628	—	1,297,100	2,758,080	4,901,549	
1795	95,362	38,421	—	1,996,320	2,626,380	6,318,812	
1796	96,460	41,592	—	2,778,000	1,182,880	7,263,539	
1797	85,109	28,746	—	3,621,260	411,240	7,869,133	Largest Ginger Crop.
1798	95,858	41,490	—	2,273,980	1,107,900	7,894,306	
1799	110,646	38,013	—	1,353,460	2,570,640	11,745,425	Bourbon Cave introduced.
1800	105,584	37,841	—	652,320	1,640,880	11,116,474	
1801	136,056	49,363		34,680	1,806,720	13,401,468	
1802	140,113	46,837	336	260,980	1,041,540	17,961,923	
1803	115,494	44,006	461	419,940	1,941,060	15,866,291	

APPENDIX B.—Contiued.

Year when exported.	Sugar. Hhds.	Rum. Punch's	Molasses. Casks.	Ginger. Pounds.	Pimento. Pounds.	Coffee. Pounds.	REMARKS.
1804	112,163	42,663	429	769,480	2,603,700	22,063,980	Largest Sugar Crop.
1805	150,352	53,950	471	412,860	940,680	24,137,393	
1806	146,601	58,780	499	460,660	2,541,000	29,298,036	
1807	135,203	52,811	699	425,320	2,401,380	26,761,188	March 25th—Abolition of Slave Trade.
1808	132,333	53,507	379	329,400	823,980	25,528,273	
1809	114,630	44,850	230	1,229,140	4,465,200	52,586,668	
1810	112,208	43,335	293	485,720	3,429,240	25,885,285	
1811	138,292	55,098	446	803,640	2,763,720	17,460,068	
1812	131,173	44,111	151	574,900	1,141,000	18,481,986	Storm in October.
1813	104,558	45,604	208	579,360	1,925,640	24,623,572	
1814	109,558	44,598	145	642,160	1,356,240	34,045,485	Largest Coffee Crop.
1815	127,269	54,321	242	946,540	3,438,240	27,362,742	Storm in Oct. 1815, that ravaged Surry.
1816	100,382	36,416	166	1,311,160	3,518,820	17,289,393	
1817	123,766	48,776	354	1,824,020	2,068,320	14,793,706	
1818	121,758	50,827	407	1,391,040	2,697,900	25,329,456	Storm in Oct. which ravaged Cornwall.
1819	116,344	45,333	253	943,160	3,098,760	14,901,983	
1820	122,922	46,983	252	617,420	1,666,740	22,127,444	
1821	119,560	47,870	167	524,520	3,199,560	16,819,761	Extreme drought this year.
1822	94,515	29,403	144	484,140	2,366,460	19,773,912	

Year						Remarks
1823	101,271	36,244	514	527,700	2,918,640	20,326,445	
1824	106,009	38,760	910	1,121,240	4,104,540	27,677,239	Mr. Canning's resolutions relative to Slavery in the West Indies.
1825	79,090	28,747	894	2,015,260	2,614,140	21,254,656	Severe drought in 1824.
1826	106,712	37,662	549	2,924,040	2,065,920	20,352,886	
1827	87,399	33,570	204	2,464,300	3,785,400	25,741,520	
1828	101,575	38,235	139	2,724,483	3,762,780	22,216,780	
1829	97,893	37,430	66	2,070,660	6,543,900	22,234,640	
1830	100,205	35,025	154	1,748,800	5,560,620	22,256,950	
1831	94,871	36,411	230	1,614,640	3,172,320	14,055,350	
1832	98,686	33,685	799	2,355,560	4,024,800	19,815,010	Largest Pimento Crop.
1833	85,401	34,976	755	2,811,760	8,423,100	9,866,060	Emancipation Act passed.
1834	84,756	32,111	486	2,976,420	3,605,400	17,725,731	Seasons favorable.
1835	67,970	27,530	300	2,050,840	7,284,660	10,593,018	,,
1836	67,094	20,536	182	2,620,280	5,654,340	13,446,053	,,
1837	61,505	21,076	173	2,759,840	5,744,220	8,955,178	
1838	69,613	25,380	149	2,567,640	2,708,640	13,551,795	Entire Emancipation, August.
1839	49,243	17,072	18	1,669,800	3,812,760	8,897,421	Seasons favorable, but the canes not taken off.
1840	36,660	11,472	18	1,400,800	3,063,980	7,279,670	
1841	34,491	11,769	51	1,834,120	3,595,380	6,433,370	Drought.
1842	50,295	16,566	109	2,008,300	3,753,960	7,048,914	,,
1843	44,169	15,046	177	1,456,725	3,546,720	7,367,113	,,
1844	34,444	11,631	92	1,993,600	1,462,440	7,148,775	Seasons favorable.
1845	47,926	16,997	15	1,888,480	7,181,220	5,021,209	Drought.
1846	36,223	14,395	76	1,462,000	2,997,060	6,047,150	Seasons favorable.
1847	48,554	18,007	22	1,324,480	2,800,140	6,421,122	Drought.
1848	42,212	20,194	2	320,340	5,231,908	6,684,941	,,

APPENDIX B.—Continued.

In making up this Tabular Return from the Records, the different Packages are thus reduced. viz.—

Sugar.	3 tierces, estimated as equal to	2 hogsheads.
	8 barrels........................	1 ditto.
Rum.	2 hogsheads.....................	1 puncheon.
	4 casks or barrels..............	1 ditto.
Ginger.	Casks as containing............	500 pounds.
	Bags...........................	120 ditto.
	Half barrels...................	250 ditto.
Pimento.	Casks as ditto.................	180 ditto.
	Casks..........................	120 ditto.

APPENDIX C.

Epitome of the Island Revenue and Expenditure for the years ending 1844, 1845, 1846, 1847, and 1848.

	To 30th Sept. 1844. (£ s. d.)	To 30th Sept. 1845. (£ s. d.)	To 30th Sept. 1846. (£ s. d.)	To 30th Sept. 1847. (£ s. d.)	To 30th Sept. 1848. (£ s. d.)
REVENUE	286,822 0 4	276,045 6 4	281,851 10 7	240,310 5 4	
SUNDRIES					
CASH IN CHEST	45,258 3 6	56,026 13 2	97,032 10 8	21,583 15 7	
EXPENDITURE,					
In collection of Revenue	31,905 17 9	32,333 3 2	34,902 12 6	31,689 11 1	25,732 3 3
Civil	79,374 6 7	76,094 12 5	73,314 16 3	66,399 11 1	57,817 4 5
Interest, annual sums to public institutions, &c	27,338 13 10	27,573 2 7	25,206 6 6	29,249 10 11	17,456 4 2
Ecclesiastical	26,768 13 10	25,944 11 6	28,081 0 10	31,671 6 1	28,214 19 8
Judicature	54,521 10 7	55,617 0 0	47,047 13 6	46,194 2 8	43,298 2 1
Military	22,374 1 4	8,920 0 6	1,577 16 6	1,627 9 9	1,174 9 4
Assembly	5,076 7 8	5,109 9 8	5,397 5 0	5,998 4 1	4,503 0 6
Government	9,642 2 8	9,488 2 0	10,053 5 6	7,837 19 2	6,480 0 0
Governor and Council		6,000 0 0	6,000 0 0	6,000 0 3	4,500 0 0
Grants, &c	7,646 16 4	10,736 16 5	8,766 4 6	20,941 19 3	
Immigration	10,804 4 6	11,145 12 9	28,331 10 10	45,507 17 8	27,053 11 8
Grants under Poll Tax	5,919 19 9	4,236 13 0	8,138 19 4	6,574 12 2	5,067 11 4
Parochial transferred to Public				4,966 13 4	14,328 10 9
	281,432 14 10	273,108 4	276,787 11	304,658 6	235,696 15 2

APPENDIX D.

In estimating the policy which England is pursuing towards the island of Jamaica, it is necessary to have in the mind some proximate notion of the magnitude and productive power of her colonial possessions, over which governmental control has to be exerted. For the convenience of my readers I have compiled the following statement of their extent, population, and resources from R. Montgomery Martin's elaborate work on " The British Colonies."

Teritorial Extent and Population.

In Asia—Bengal, Madras, Bombay, Scinde, the N. W. provinces of Hindostan, the Punjaub, Assam, Arracan, Savoy, Tenasserim, Wellesley Province, and Malacca; the Islands of Ceylon, Penang, Singapore, Labuan, Hong-Kong; area, (in round numbers,) seven hundred thousand square miles; population about one hundred and twelve million. In addition to this territory actually belonging to the British crown in Asia, there are tributary states, extending over half a million square miles, and containing more than fifty million people.

In North America.—The Canadas, (Upper and Lower,) Nova Scotia, New Brunswick, and Cape Breton, and the Islands of Prince Edward, Newfoundland, and Vancouver's and Queen Charlotte; with an area of more than half a million of square miles, and two millions inhabitants. We have also on the continent of North America, the territories belonging to and under the control of, the Hudson's Bay Company, extending from the northern frontier of Canada to the Frozen Ocean, and from the Atlantic to the Pacific, which comprises upwards of three millions square miles, and a population of about one hundred and twenty thousand.

In South America.—Demarara, Essequibo, and Berbice; Honduras and the Falkland Islands. Area about two hundred thousand square miles, population one hundred and fifty thousand.

In the West Indies.—The Islands of Jamaica, the Caymans, Trinidad, Tobago, Barbadoes, St. Vincents, Grenada, Antigua, St. Lucia, Dominica, St. Christophers, Nevis, Montserrat, Anguilla, Tortola, and the Virgin Islands, Providence and the Bahamas, and the Bermudas. Area about twenty thousand square miles; population nearly one million.

In Africa.—The Cape of Good Hope and Natal, the the Mauritius and Seychelle Islands, Aden, (in Arabia,) Sierra Leone, the Gambia, Cape Coast Castle, Accra, and

Annamaboe, the Islands of St. Helena and Ascension. Area four hundred thousand square miles; population eight hundred thousand.

In AUSTRALIA.—The great Island of Australia, or New Holland, which contains the settlements of New South Wales, Port Philip, South Australia, Western Australia or Swan River, Northern Australia or Port Essington, Van Dieman's Island, New Zealand, Norfolk Island, and the Auchland Islands. Area more than three million square miles; population half a million, of whom 325,000 are Europeans and their descendants.

In EUROPE.—Gibraltar, Malta, Gozo, Corfu, Cephalonia, Zante, Santa Maura, Ithaca, and Cerigo in the Mediterranean, and Heligoland in the German Ocean. Jersey, Guernsey, Alderney, and Sark, have been held as fiefs of the Crown since the reign of William the Conqueror. The area of these territories and dependencies is about fifteen hundred square miles; population nearly half a million.

Total area, *eight million* square miles; population about *one hundred and twenty million.* * * * *

In British North America there are about two million white inhabitants, of whom six hundred thousand are of French descent, and the remainder of the Anglo-Saxon race. There are also about one hundred thousand Indians in the territories confided to the management of the Hudson's Bay Company.

In South Africa, the British subjects are Dutch, English, Hottentots, Caffres, &c. At the Isle of France and Seychelles, principally French; at Aden, Arabs; on the west coast of Africa, negroes.

In Australia there are about three hundred and twenty-five thousand of the Anglo-Saxon race, and no other European blood; there are probably one hundred thousand New Zealanders, a fine race; and scattered savage hordes in Australia. At Gibraltar there is a medley of many Mediterranean and African races. At Malta, a peculiar population, partaking of the characteristics of the various nations under whose dominion the island has passed. In the Ionian Islands, the inhabitants are principally Greek, with some Venetian blood; in Heligoland, Germans, and in the Norman, or Channel Islands, French. The languages spoken throughout the British empire, are English, French, Italian, Dutch, Spanish, Portuguese, Greek, Persian, Arabic, Maltese, Chinese, Armenian, Hindoostanee, Bengallee, Mahratti, Tamul, Teloogoo, Carnatica, Ooria, Singale, Malay, Burmese or Assamese, Hottentot, Kaffre, Negro, New Zealand, and various barbarous unwritten tongues. There are about 5,000,000 Christians in our foreign possessions, including the Lutheran, Latin, Greek, and Syrian Churches. There are about 50,000,000 Hindoos, professing the religion of Brahm or Brahma; about 20,000,000 Mohammedans; about

10,000,000 Budhists or Jains, a small number of the Zoroaster creed, and the remainder are idolaters of various descriptions.   *   *   *   *   *   *   *

Estimating the whole population of the British empire at 130,000,000, not more than 26,000,000 consume flesh abundantly ; about 10,000,000 eat of it sparingly; 24,000,000 occasionally partake of it, and 70,000,000 live principally on vegetables and fish. Wheat, oats, and barley constitute the principle gramnivorous food of about 34,000,000 ; potatoes, pulse, and other vegetables, of about 16,000,000; and rice, maize, millet and several minor grains, of about 80,000,000 people. With regard to fermented or distilled drink, about 10,000,000 use wine frequently, 25,000,000 malt liquors, 35,000,000 distilled liquors, and about 60,000,000 confine themselves chiefly to aqueous beverages. About one half the population of the British empire reside within the temperate, and the other half within the torrid zone.   *   *   *   *

The whole sums voted by Parliament for the *civil expenditure* of the colonies in 1849, derived from the revenues of Great Britain, were, in round numbers—Bahamas, £300 ; Bermuda, £4,000 ; Prince Edward Island, £2,-000 ; Western Coast of Africa, £13,000 ; Western Australia, £7,400 ; Port Essington, or Northern Australia, (about to be abandoned,) £1,700 ; New Zealand, £20,-000 ; Heligoland, £1,000 ; Falkland Islands, £5,700 ;

Hong Kong, £28,000; Labuan, £10,000; Governors and others in the West Indies, £18,000; St. Helena and retired servants of East India Company, £17,000. *Total*, £128,000. Clergy in North America, £11,500; Indian Department, Canada, £14,000; Justices or Stipendiary Magistrates in the West Indies, Mauritius, &c., £41,000; Militia and volunteers in Canada, £6,000; Emigration department, £13,000; Colonial office, £37,000. *Total*, £133,000. Thus, it will be seen, that the total civil charges of the whole of our colonies defrayed out of the home exchequer, directly or indirectly, permanently or temporarily, is about a quarter of a million sterling.

The people of British India provide *the whole* of the civil and military charges of Hindoostan, defray annually the expenses of twenty to thirty thousand of the Queen's troops; the cost of the Court of Directors of the East India Company in Leadenhall street, and of the India Board in Westminster. The convict expenditure in Australia and Bermuda, is about £225,000 a year, but this outlay results from vice and crime in the United Kingdom, and is not chargeable to our colonies. The total military cost for the pay and commissariat of the Queen's troops in all our colonies was, for the year 1847, say, £1,503,059, commissariat, £670,142—£2,174,059. Of this sum, £603,718 was for the Cape of Good Hope, during the Caffre war. In some of the colonies there are local corps, as in tl

West Indies, Ceylon and Malta. There are militia corps in several of our settlements; those of our North American colonies compose 339,139 men.   *   *   *

* * * The shipping registered as sailing vessels in the British colonies in North America, Australia, Africa and the West Indies, amounts to half a million tons, and the steam vessels to sixteen thousand tons. The British shipping cleared out of the ports of the United Kingdom, for the British possessions alone, in 1847, amounted to more than 2,000,000 tons.

* * * Of 7,000,000 cwt. of sugar imported, our colonies furnish 5,500,000. They send us also 35,000,000 lbs. of coffee, 4,000,000 lbs. of cocoa, 7,000 gallons of rum, 1,000,000 lbs. of cinnamon, 13,000,000 lbs. pepper, 2,000,000 galls. of vegetable oils, 8,000,000 lbs. of indigo, 40,000,000 lbs. of wool, (sheep) 100,000,000 lbs. of cotton wool, 1,000,000 lbs. of silk, 1,000,000 cwt. of rice, 1,000,000 loads of timber, also corn, provisions, flax, hemp, hides, skins, saltpetre, gums, drugs, dyes, metals, &c., all capable of indefinite increase. In fish alone, Newfoundland has contributed to the empire to the value of about £200,000,000, a richer wealth than the South American mines yielded to Spain.

The exports of manufactured articles from the United Kingdom, to the colonies, nearly equals our whole exports of similar articles to every part of the globe. Mr. D'Israeli

stated in Parliament on July 2d, 1849, " that in the article
of Calicoes alone, there has been an export to the British
colonies, from 1831 to 1836, of 313,000,000 yards more
than to all the rest of the world," and it must be remem-
bered that a colonial trade is even more valuable than a
home trade, because not only are the two profits on buying and selling obtained by the citizens of the same empire, but a larger and valuable amount of shipping is employed.

British India and Ceylon consume annually British and
Irish produce and manufactures of the value of £6,000,000.
North American colonies £4,500,000; West Indies
£3,500,000; Australian colonies £2,000,000; the African Settlements more than £2,000,000; the European
and other Settlements require for use or sale about
£2,000,000. Our colonial export trade therefore, amounts
to £20,000,000 a year, and is annually increasing. This
commerce, in a national point of view, is double the value
of an equal amount of foreign commerce, for the reasons
above stated; namely, that the whole profits thereon ac-
crue to the empire, and are in no way divided with foreign
States.

JOHN BIGELOW (1817-1911) was an editor at the New York Evening Post and an early organizer of the Free-Soil Party.

ROBERT J. SCHOLNICK is a professor of English and American studies and the founding director of the American Studies Program at the College of William and Mary. His books include American Literature and Science and Edmund Clarence Stedman. He is at work on a study of American debates over evolution before Darwin.

The University of Illinois Press
is a founding member of the
Association of American University Presses.

University of Illinois Press
1325 South Oak Street
Champaign, IL 61820-6903
www.press.uillinois.edu